What Nietzsche Really Said

Mazzino Montinari (1928–86) was an Italian philologist and leading Nietzsche scholar. Best known for his collaboration with Giorgio Colli on the critical edition of Nietzsche's works, Montinari dedicated his career to restoring Nietzsche's writings to their authentic form, free from distortions by Nazi and doctrinaire interpretations.

Peter J. Schwartz is associate professor of German and comparative literature and film in the Department of World Languages and Literatures at Boston University. His work turns primarily on matters of verbal and visual expression, social and aesthetic distinction, cultural history and morphology, and media archaeology. He is the author of *After Jena: Goethe's Elective Affinities and the End of the Old Regime*, co-editor of *Labour in a Single Shot: Critical Perspectives on Antje Ehmann and Harun Farocki's Global Video Project* and translator of André Jolles's *Simple Forms*.

What Nietzsche Really Said

A Reader's Guide

Mazzino Montinari

Translated with a Foreword by Peter J. Schwartz

VERSO
London • New York

The English-language edition first published by Verso 2026
First published as *Che cosa ha 'veramente' detto Nietzsche* (Ubaldini) 1975
Subsequently published as *Che cosa ha detto Nietzsche*

The manufacturer's authorized representative in the EU for product safety (GPSR) is LOGOS EUROPE, 9 rue Nicolas Poussin, 17000, La Rochelle, France
contact@logoseurope.eu

1 3 5 7 9 10 8 6 4 2

Verso
UK: 6 Meard Street, London W1F 0EG
US: 207 East 32nd Street, New York, NY 10016
versobooks.com

Verso is the imprint of New Left Books

ISBN-13: 978-1-80429-501-4
ISBN-13: 978-1-80429-503-8 (US EBK)
ISBN-13: 978-1-80429-502-1 (UK EBK)

British Library Cataloguing in Publication Data
A catalogue record for this book is available from the British Library

Library of Congress Cataloging-in-Publication Data

Names: Montinari, Mazzino author | Schwartz, Peter J., 1967– translator
Title: What Nietzsche really said : a reader's guide / Mazzino Montinari ; translated with an introduction by Peter J. Schwartz.
Other titles: Che cosa ha detto Nietzsche. English
Description: First edition paperback. | London ; New York : Verso, [2026] | 'The English-language edition first published by Verso 2026. First published as Che cosa ha 'veramente' detto Nietzsche© Ubaldini 1975' – Title page verso | Includes bibliographical references and index.
Identifiers: LCCN 2026025528 (print) | LCCN 2026025529 (ebook) | ISBN 9781804295014 paperback | ISBN 9781804295038 ebk
Classification: LCC B3316 .M713 2026 (print) | LCC B3316 (ebook)
LC record available at https://lccn.loc.gov/2026025528
LC ebook record available at https://lccn.loc.gov/2026025529

Typeset in Fournier by Hewer Text UK Ltd, Edinburgh
Printed and bound by CPI Group (UK) Ltd, Croydon, CR0 4YY

Contents

Mazzino Montinari
(photo by Isolde Ohlbaum)

Foreword: Mazzino Montinari and *Che cosa ha 'veramente' detto Nietzsche* (1975)

Mazzino Montinari (1928–86) was a founding editor, with Giorgio Colli, of the now standard 'historical-critical' edition of Nietzsche's writings and letters, published concurrently in Italian, French, German and Japanese beginning in 1964.[1] His book *Che cosa ha 'veramente' detto Nietzsche* (*What Nietzsche 'Really' Said*, later shortened to *Che cosa ha detto Nietzsche*),[2] the fruit of some

---

1 *Kritische Gesamtausgabe Werke* (KGW): Italian (Adelphi, 1964 ff.), French (Gallimard, 1965 ff.), German (De Gruyter, 1967 ff.), Japanese (Hakusuisha, 1979 ff.); *Kritische Gesamtausgabe Briefe* (KGB): Italian (Adelphi, 1977 ff.), French (Gallimard, 1986 ff.), German (De Gruyter, 1975 ff.). There are also incomplete Spanish and English editions based on the KGW published by Editorial Technos (2003 ff.), Cambridge University Press (1983 ff.) and Stanford University Press (1995 ff.). I would like to thank Silvia Beier, Raymond Geuss, Nancy Harrowitz, Paul Katsafanas, Brian Leiter, Matthew Wilson Smith, James Uden and W. Daniel Wilson for advice and encouragement, Tim Clark for able copy-editing and Sebastian Budgen and Mark Martin for seeing this project through the editorial process.

2 The book was initially published by Ubaldini in 1975 under the title *Che cosa ha 'veramente' detto Nietzsche* as part of a series of short introductions to what selected philosophers had 'really' said. The title was shortened to *Che cosa ha detto Nietzsche* when Adelphi acquired the book in 1999.

fifteen years of intensive engagement with Nietzsche's *Nachlass* in the Goethe and Schiller Archive in Weimar, echoes the rationale of the critical edition in attempting to extricate Nietzsche from his postwar reputation as a 'spiritual ancestor of fascism' by representing his thought in all the contingent complexity of its historical development. 'Our edition has a prehistory,' Montinari wrote in an essay of 1980:

> It was in the small medieval city of Lucca that we – a small group of high-school students – first heard Nietzsche's name spoken by our beloved philosophy teacher, Giorgio Colli. At that time, in 1943, he was 26 years old and was trying to guide us through the 'stubble fields' of philology so as to give us a sense of classical Greek philosophy. From him we also learned opposition to fascism. The best of us entered combat for freedom, while many of us were expelled from school for participating in an antifascist demonstration. Colli, our philosophy teacher, had to repair to Switzerland. In the dark years 1943–44 the expelled students often met at my house, where we worked out new ways of vexing the fascists. On our own and with the help of other antifascist teachers we also managed to study a bit, reading and discussing passages from Plato, from Kant – and *Thus Spoke Zarathustra*. Why am I recounting all this? To make clear that the bad (because ideological) equation 'Nietzsche = fascism' was invalid for us. Our relationship with Nietzsche remained essentially uncompromised, even after the war was over and Nietzsche fell victim, in Germany, to the work of denazification.[3]

3 Mazzino Montinari, 'Prologo', *Su Nietzsche* (Rome: Editori Riuniti, 1981), 3–4. Translated as 'The New Critical Edition of Nietzsche's Works', in Mazzino Montinari, *Reading Nietzsche*, trans. Greg Whitlock (Champaign: University of Illinois Press, 2003), 13–22.

In Montinari's and Colli's account, Nietzsche's nazification – the concerted enlistment of bastardized versions of his philosophy and mythical constructions of his biography in the service of National Socialist ideology, as well as his postwar rejection by left intellectuals as ideologically unredeemable – was due, in large part, to an archival history deformed by the efforts of Nietzsche's sister Elisabeth to shape his legacy following his collapse into madness in January 1889. Returning to Germany in 1893 after a failed attempt to found a nationalist German colony in Paraguay with her antisemitic husband Bernhard Förster, Elisabeth spent decades tailoring a mythic image of her brother and his work to suit a budding Nietzsche cult centred in Weimar. Having gained legal control of Nietzsche's literary estate, she founded an archive, published a biography and an edition of his collected writings, and invited admirers to pay her and her brother court, first at the family's house in Naumburg and then in the Weimar villa where Nietzsche would die in 1900 and where his papers were housed until 1950, when they were removed to the nearby Goethe and Schiller Archive. Although Elisabeth was by no means the only architect either of Nietzsche's cult status or of his image as a bellicose German nationalist, still her archive would prove a hospitable place for fascist ideology, its editorial programme being well suited to Nietzsche's official promotion as fascism's intellectual ancestor.[4]

---

4 Robert C. Holub rejects the postwar assignment of blame to Elisabeth Förster-Nietzsche for what fascism would make of Nietzsche as a convenient legend, objecting that 'Nietzsche has been consistently extricated from his Nazi entanglements by regarding Elisabeth as the chief architect of his fascist reputation.' Holub also disputes that Elisabeth was herself antisemitic. Robert C. Holub, 'The Elisabeth Legend: The Cleansing of Nietzsche and the Sullying of His Sister', in Jacob Golomb and Robert S. Wistrich, eds., *Nietzsche, Godfather of Fascism? On the Uses and Abuses of History* (Princeton, NJ: Princeton University Press, 2002), 221 and 228–30.

By 1932, Elisabeth and all her employees were enthusiastic Nazis; a visit by Hitler in 1934 and his attendance the following year at her funeral were duly turned to propagandistic account.[5] In July 1943, Hitler would send Mussolini, then in captivity on the island of Ponza, a specially bound edition of Nietzsche's works for his sixtieth birthday – which, unlike Hitler, Mussolini had already read.[6]

For Montinari and Colli, Elisabeth's most consequential delicts were philological, consisting, above all, in distortions of Nietzsche's biography supported by censored, doctored and fabricated documents and in editorial falsifications of unpublished writings, especially the collection of posthumous fragments first published in 1901 under the title *The Will to Power*, a text touted by Nazi ideologues as a *summa* of Nietzsche's philosophy but proven by Montinari to have been mostly a fabrication from posthumous fragments.[7] Elisabeth's censorship and falsification of

---

5 Steven E. Aschheim, *The Nietzsche Legacy in Germany 1890–1990* (Berkeley: University of California Press, 1992), 239–40.

6 Philipp Felsch, *How Nietzsche Came in From the Cold: Tale of a Redemption*, trans. Daniel Bowles (Cambridge: Polity, 2024), 13; Karl Pestalozzi, 'Laudatio auf Mazzino Montinari,' *Nietzsche-Studien. Internationales Jahrbuch für die Nietzsche-Forschung: Gedenkband für Mazzino Montinari*, ed. Ernst Behler, Wolfgang Müller-Lauter and Heinz Wenzel, 18 (1989): 28.

7 Alfred Bäumler's afterword to the 1930 Kröner edition begins: 'The "Will to Power" is Nietzsche's principal philosophical work. All the fundamental results of his thinking are united in this book. One must not be kept by the author's dislike for systems from calling this work a system. Nietzsche scorned only the construction of artificial, logical-closed systems; otherwise he knew very well that all truly philosophical thinking is systematic: that is, that it has a generative centre that determines and supports the particulars.' Alfred Bäumler, 'Nachwort', in Friedrich Nietzsche, *Der Wille zur Macht. Versuch einer Umwertung aller Werte* (Leipzig: Alfred Kröner Verlag, 1930), 699. As Montinari points out, the legitimacy of the text established in 1901 by Elisabeth

information pertaining to Nietzsche's final illness in an attempt to evade the familial shame of a hereditary taint, her withholding from publication and possible destruction of documents that did not assort with the image she wished to purvey of her brother, the tendentious inaccuracy of her multivolume biography (1895–1906), all come in for deft and acerbic critique in Montinari's book, as do the mystifications of 'Nietzscheans' writing in her wake such as Ernst Bertram, author of the influential *Nietzsche: Attempt at a Mythology* (1918), or the Nazi ideologue Alfred Bäumler, the 'official writer of prefaces to Nietzsche's works in the 1930s', whose edition of *The Will to Power* would remain in print, with Bäumler's name and afterword eventually removed, until 2001.[8]

Förster-Nietzsche and Nietzsche's friend Peter Gast was first put into question in 1906–7 by two editors of the expanded and substantially reordered edition of 1906, August and Ernst Horneffer, and then again in 1956 by Richard Roos and Karl Schlechta. Montinari, *Su Nietzsche*, 8 and 81 and this volume, 136. Curiously, although the American scholar Walter Kaufmann rejected the construction of *The Will to Power* as Nietzsche's *magnum opus* in 1964, declaring Förster-Nietzsche's edition at best a useful source 'for those who realized that these were merely notes' (Walter Kaufmann, *Nietzsche: Philosopher, Psychologist, Antichrist*, 4th ed. [Princeton, NJ: Princeton University Press, 1974], 442), in 1967 he published a full English translation of the book. Cf. Giuliano Campioni, *Leggere Nietzsche. Alle origini dell'edizione critica Colli-Montinari, con lettere e testi inediti* (Pisa: ETS Editrice, 1992), 385n71. One of Montinari's earliest reports to Colli from the archive in Weimar (21 August 1961) already shows him testing Schlechta's doubts against Nietzsche's manuscripts (Campioni, *Leggere Nietzsche*, 74–5, 261–5 and 262n13).

8 Montinari, 'Delio Cantimori e Nietzsche', *Su Nietzsche*, 110–12 on Bertram (and Thomas Mann). Bäumler's name and afterword are still on and in the twelfth edition of 1980, replaced by Walter Gebhard on the thirteenth edition in 1996 (last reprinted 2001). Gebhard claims in his afterword (705) to have checked the text against the KGW, but to have retained Bäumler's

The chief intent of the new historical-critical edition was to disengage the philosopher and his work from such appropriation by providing readers with a complete and accurate record of what Nietzsche really wrote, including all extant published and unpublished texts, fragments and letters, transcribed in their integral form and set clearly within the biographical and historical context of their production. This, too, is the task of *Che cosa ha detto Nietzsche*: to insulate Nietzsche from ideological distortion by presenting the written record of his thinking as a matter of contingent and often unresolved development over time within definite historical contexts, not as the finished realization of a systematic philosophical programme. In so doing, Montinari invites the reader into the sort of careful reading espoused by the philologically trained Nietzsche himself:

> For philology is that venerable art which demands of its votaries one thing above all: to go aside, to take time, to become still, to become slow – it is a goldsmith's art and connoisseurship of the word which has nothing but delicate, cautious work to do and achieves nothing if it does not achieve it *lento*. But for precisely this reason it is more necessary than ever today, by precisely this means does it entice and enchant us the most, in the midst of an age of 'work', that is to say, of hurry, of indecent and perspiring haste, which wants to 'get everything done' at once, including every old or new book: – this art does not so easily get anything done, it teaches to read well, that is to say, to read slowly, deeply, looking cautiously before and aft,

---

selection and ordering of the material. See David Marc Hoffmann, *Zur Geschichte des Nietzsche-Archivs. Elisabeth Förster-Nietzsche, Fritz Koegel, Rudolf Steiner, Gustav Naumann, Josef Hofmiller. Chronik, Studien und Dokumente* (Berlin: De Gruyter, 1991), 102–3, 109, 129.

> with reservations, with doors left open, with delicate eyes and fingers . . . My patient friends, this book [*Daybreak*] desires for itself only perfect readers and philologists: *learn* to read me well![9]

Montinari's postwar political alignment with the Italian Communist Party (PCI), of which he remained a culturally active member until the Soviet intervention in the Hungarian Revolution of 1956, compelled a reckoning not only with ideologues on the right, but also with those on the left. The Nazis' reduction to militant catchwords of such Nietzschean concepts as the will to power, the *Übermensch* and the 'blonde beast'; their amplification of Nietzsche's (undeniable) antidemocratic, antisocialist and eugenicist moments and studied neglect of the writings in which he espoused cosmopolitanism, enlightenment and individualism or scorned Germans, nationalists and antisemites while praising Jews for their cultural value and intellectual acuity; the Nazi mythical construction of Nietzsche as a tragic Wagnerian hero, a philosophical Siegfried – all this would produce an equally reductive image of Nietzsche in postwar Italian and German Marxist and Socialist discourse and an effective taboo on his thought in left-wing circles, while, in East Germany, his stylization as an arch-enemy of socialism rendered his archive off-limits to researchers from countries in the Soviet bloc and prevented republication of his works.[10] Most influential was the Hungarian

9 *Daybreak: Thoughts on the Prejudices of Morality*, ed. Maudemarie Clarke and Brian Leiter, trans. R. J. Hollingdale (Cambridge: Cambridge University Press, 1997), 5. Footnote to text. The word 'reading' appears in the titles of many texts by and about Montinari, including his late essay 'L'honorevole arte di leggere Nietzsche', *Belfagor* 41.3 (1986): 335–40.

10 'Nietzsche was officially proscribed within East Germany and tabooed as the primary philosopher of a brutalized German fascism.' Aschheim, *The*

Marxist György Lukács, whose book *Die Zerstörung der Vernunft* (*The Destruction of Reason*, 1954, later subtitled *The Way of Irrationalism from Schelling to Hitler*) construed a chain of intellectual and ideological debt stretching from German romantic philosophy through Nietzsche and Oswald Spengler to National Socialism, with Nietzsche as a key link in the chain. Montinari's and Colli's task, as they saw it, was to provide readers with the means to dissociate Nietzsche's work not only from its Nazi caricature but also from Lukács's deployment of that very caricature as an ideological straw man. As Colli put it in his prospectus of 1963 for the Italian edition of the collected works: 'Nietzsche became a phantasm, and then the execrations of those who replaced the ones who exalted him were turned against the phantasm.'[11]

Lukács's teleological and retrospective approach, his attempt to explain Nazism as an outgrowth of characteristic national attitudes and prior German cultural trends, is shared by such other works of the moment as Siegfried Kracauer's *From Caligari to Hitler: A Psychological History of the German Film* (1947) and Thomas Mann's novel *Doctor Faustus: The Life of the German Composer Adrian Leverkühn as Told to a Friend* (1947), which both

---

Nietzsche Legacy, 304, citing Dennis M. Sweet, 'Friedrich Nietzsche in the GDR: A Problematic Reception', *Studies in GDR Culture and Society* 4 (1984): 224–41.

11 Giorgio Colli, 'Premessa', *Scritti su Nietzsche* (Milan: Adelphi, 1980), 12–13. Montinari also observes that, for all his polemical sallies against socialism, Nietzsche never read a word of Marx and never mentions him by name, a fact that undercuts Lukács's reading of his work as 'one continuous polemic against Marxism, against socialism'. Montinari, 'Equivoci marxisti', *Su Nietzsche*, 90–103, here 94. On Montinari's relationship to Lukács (whose *Prolegomena to a Marxist Aesthetics* he translated in 1957), see Giuliano Campioni, 'Mazzino Montinari in den Jahren von 1943 bis 1963', *Nietzsche-Studien* 17 (1988): xxvi.

undertook anamneses of the intellectual and psychological states presumed to have led up to fascism. Whereas Kracauer sought cinematic evidence of German interwar 'mental attitudes' to explain the failure of middle-class Germans to recognize the convergence of their own interests not with the Nazis but with the political left, Mann articulated the complex weave of the German cultural fabric from which fascism had been cut as the fictional biography of a composer himself woven of those strands, as Mann also felt himself to be: above all, of elements of Nietzsche's life and work, of Beethoven's music and of the Faust tradition. Indeed, Montinari's choice of *Germanistik* as a vocation – aside from his life's work with Nietzsche, he would translate and write about Mann, Goethe, Heinrich Heine, Freud, Marx and Engels, Schopenhauer, Jacob Burckhardt, and Robert Musil, and teach at the universities of Urbino and Florence and at the Free University in Berlin – was initially sparked by Mann's book-length account of the writing of *Doctor Faustus*, *The Story of a Novel* (1949), which Montinari first encountered while doing Party work in East Berlin in June 1953.[12] Although the brutal repression, with Soviet tanks, of a citywide general strike on 17 June accelerated the disillusionment with Stalinism that would eventually lead Montinari to leave the PCI after the Hungarian uprising of October–November 1956, in February 1957 he co-founded an Italian institute for German studies in Rome, the Centro Thomas Mann, whose main purpose – supported by East German government funding – was to promote cultural exchange between Italy and the GDR.[13]

---

12 Giorgio Montinari, 'Gli anni dell'impegno', in Adriano Montinari, ed., *Coraggio dell'intelligenza: Mazzino Montinari* (Pisa: Edizioni ETS, 2023), 44.

13 Ibid., 49. Campioni, 'Mazzino Montinari in den Jahren von 1943 bis 1963', xxv; see also Alessandro Fambrini, 'Mazzino Montinari, ovvero della

This shift from direct political activity to a carefully non-ideological cultural activism characterizes Montinari's approach to Nietzsche, who became his intellectual focus following a reunion with Colli at the funeral of a friend and former classmate, Angelo Pasquinelli, in June 1956.[14] It also informs Montinari's high opinion of Nietzsche's colleague and friend, the Basel historian Jacob Burckhardt, whose distinction of culture from the political sphere of the state is the moral and methodological centre of *Che cosa ha detto Nietzsche*. For Montinari, as (in his estimation) for Nietzsche, 'the perspective of "culture" (*Kultur*) is decisive . . . by "culture" [Nietzsche] means what Burckhardt, too, had been expounding in his lectures on the study of history . . . a power essentially antagonistic to the state, and in general to all established public powers'.[15] Montinari's book ends with an overt rejection of ideological assimilation in favour of free and open cultural engagement in this sense with Nietzsche's thinking, in all its complexity:

> it is not a question of wanting to 'recover Nietzsche for democracy and socialism' . . . but rather of asserting that even within a socialist and democratic society (or within the movement that could lead to one) we cannot do without a 'Nietzsche dimension' – that is, without the dimension of mental freedom

---

filologia e dell'impegno', and Giorgio Montinari, 'Gli anni dell'impegno', in Adriano Montinari, ed., *Coraggio dell'intelligenza*, 16 and 48, and Felsch, *How Nietzsche Came in From the Cold*, 69–71.

14 Montinari, 'Gli anni dell'impegno', 49; Felsch, *How Nietzsche Came in from the Cold*, 78–9. See also Sossio Giametta, *Colli, Montinari e Nietzsche* (Milan: Book Time, 2018), 95–7, on the political commitment implied in Montinari's practice of philology.

15 This volume, 60.

> born of the critical, rational and liberatory potential of his thought, which never tires of putting everything into question. This also permits us to ask whether the individual (even in a society of presumptive equals) properly finds his defence and his own field of spontaneous activity in the realm of culture (as Burckhardt also understood it), and, in the last analysis, *against the state* – provided that one believes in the necessary extinction of the state in the 'reign of freedom', and that one thus really desires the overcoming of 'politics' as repression.[16]

Montinari's historical-philological disinclination to understand Nietzsche's philosophy as a system set him productively at odds with his former teacher and co-editor Colli, whose preoccupation with Nietzsche (as with the philosophy of the ancient Greeks, about which he wrote several books) was driven principally by a desire to model on them a life lived philosophically in the present. The teacher–student relationship developed with Montinari and others at the Ginnasio Machiavelli in Lucca in 1943–4 adapted a Platonic conception of Greek *paideia* in tacit opposition to the

---

16 This volume, 154. Giametta questions the possibility of maintaining the culture/politics distinction (*Colli, Montinari e Nietzsche*, 105–7). An English translation of the text in which this distinction was theorized, Burckhardt's *Weltgeschichtiche Betrachtungen* (*Observations on World History*), a posthumous publication of 1905 (expanded edition, Zurich 1941) based on notes for lectures of 1868–71 that Nietzsche attended at Basel, was produced in 1943 by Pantheon Books, the New York publishing house of the German émigrés Kurt and Helen Wolff, under the title *Force and Freedom*. The jacket copy is explicit about the edition's intended relevance to current events: 'Almost alone among nineteenth-century historians, Jacob Burckhardt saw the totalitarian direction that history would take in our own century. This book contains the quintessence of Burckhardt's political wisdom and is a guide to the study and comprehension of historical processes.'

neo-Hegelian Idealism of orthodox Fascist pedagogy under Mussolini's Minister of Education Giovanni Gentile, which subsumed the project of philosophical education to the ideological requirement of proving the Fascist state the legitimate realization of the world-historical progress of philosophical reason.[17] In his performative insistence at Lucca on the autonomous value of philosophical discourse, Colli, too, aimed at an 'overcoming of politics' by adhering to Burckhardt's distinction between the sphere of culture and that of the State. Montinari's approach to Nietzsche, however, differed from Colli's in ways that compelled Montinari – nine years Colli's junior and attached to him by strong bonds of love, gratitude and respect – continually to question, define and defend his own methods and motivations, a process that can be traced in his letters to Colli from Weimar during the years 1961–70.[18] The philosopher and translator Sossio Giametta, who along with another young assistant, Maria Ludovica Pampaloni, worked in the archive with Montinari between 1962 and 1965, summarized their differences thus:[19]

> Colli was a visionary, a 'hunter of being' with a tendency toward mysticism, and, like his beloved Schopenhauer, antipathetic to history; Montinari, on the other hand, fully incarnated the critical and historical teachings of the man who, after Colli at the lyceum in Lucca, had been his second and formative master at the University of Pisa, Delio Cantimori. Montinari was driven by a moral inspiration (Colli's inspiration was cosmic), which had drawn him toward an active interest in politics and to militancy as a functionary in the Italian Communist Party; he had a

17 Felsch, *How Nietzsche Came in From the Cold*, 14–15.

18 Published in Campioni, *Leggere Nietzsche*.

19 Ibid., 113–14, 373n62.

> faith in enlightenment and a social passion which always remained the foundation of his interpretation of Nietzsche.[20]

A letter to Colli of 11 November 1963, after some two and a half years in the archive, partly captures the tone and the tension of their relationship:

> For me Nietzsche is becoming a great test, I feel myself continually called to take a position, and at this point all I want is to arrive at an understanding of him, that is: to make him mine. I don't know how to tell you how much with every passing day this work becomes ever more my own, *because it is my torment*. It is by tormenting myself with the richness and splendour, but also the misery, the disorientation, the sickness of *all* of Nietzsche that I would achieve *my* position with regard to him. And I am grateful to you for having made this work possible for me, which is *our* work now. And if you should think the worst of me, if you should feel hostile towards me: I am not forgetting how much, besides this present gift of friendship (working on the edition), how much I have always *taken* from you. I feel this so much that I am unable to see if I have given you anything.[21]

Some four years later, he confesses again to a certain 'repugnance at taking positions' that causes him difficulty in

---

20 Giametta, *Colli, Montinari e Nietzsche*, 9; see also 134–5.

21 Campioni, *Leggere Nietzsche*, 291–2, emphasis in original. See also page 79: 'He was becoming convinced of a kind of historical knowledge that would be open to the plural nature of reality and decidedly alien to the certainties of dogma, but also to those of the "strong" philosophy of his friend [Colli].'

formulating 'philosophical' (rather than philological) arguments about Nietzsche, and remarks that he has the impression that Colli is experiencing their editorial work as a burden (there is evidence too of impatience with Montinari's philological meticulousness),[22] tempering the tension each time with heartfelt apologies: 'Excuse me if you can for my intemperance, for the sudden outburst. I take it all back. And it isn't true that I feel you only partly understand me. The truth is that we have a difficult battle to fight together, in which conflicts will inevitably arise, and which each of us will have to fight in a way that's consistent with our character.'[23] When Colli died of an aneurysm in 1979, Montinari was devastated.[24]

The historian Delio Cantimori, with whom Montinari studied at Pisa in 1945–49 (writing a master's thesis within one of Cantimori's fields of interest, on the Protestant Reformation in sixteenth-century Lucca), and with whom he remained in close friendly contact until Cantimori's death in September 1966, figured for Montinari as a methodological beacon in his work on Nietzsche and as a counterweight to Colli's antihistorical

22 Ibid., 144–5 (Letter of 16 November 1965), 434 (Letter of 10 September 1967); Giametta, *Colli, Montinari e Nietzsche*, 86 and 135–6; Felsch, *How Nietzsche Came in From the Cold*, 121.

23 Letter of 3 March 1967, in Campioni, *Leggere Nietzsche*, 409. See also letters of 13 February and 7 May 1967, pp. 402 and 417. Indeed, most of Montinari's own writing arose in service of his philological work, e.g. as introductions to editions or translations or as short assessments of the relationships between Nietzsche and such figures as Burckhardt, Richard Wagner and Lou Andreas-Salomé, or his reception by Cantimori, Mann, Bäumler and Lukács. Cf. Giametta, *Colli, Montinari e Nietzsche*, 95.

24 Felsch, *How Nietzsche Came in From the Cold*, 218n9.

temperament.[25] His description of Cantimori's approach to Nietzsche is programmatic for his own work:

> The correct distinction between the temporal coordinates of an author, on the one hand, that is the questions to which he wanted to respond, and his actualization or utilization in subsequent periods (or in contiguous but different environments), on the other, without forgetting the historically verifiable relationship between the author and his fortunes, between the texts in their original historicity and their deferred readings at later moments, this distinction and this sense of diversity within continuity seems to me constantly present whenever Cantimori speaks of Nietzsche or Nietzscheanism.[26]

Cantimori's personal trajectory from fascism in the late 1920s and early 1930s to communism by the end of the '30s – he would become a member of the PCI in 1948 and translate Marx's *Capital* in 1951–52, before leaving the Party, like Montinari, in 1956 – occupies a place in some ways analogous to that of Thomas Mann in Montinari's reflections on Nietzsche's political reception. In an essay of 1979 on Cantimori and Nietzsche, Montinari relates Cantimori's engagement in the early 1930s with Ernst Bertram's *Nietzsche: Attempt at a Mythology* (1918) to Mann's friendship with Bertram (which ended in 1933, when Bertram began making public pronouncements supporting Hitler) and to his fascination

25 Campioni, *Leggere Nietzsche*, 25–9; Felsch, *How Nietzsche Came in From the Cold*, 54–61; and Giametta, *Colli, Montinari e Nietzsche*, 134–5, on Colli's resentment of Cantimori, and 142–5 on Montinari's allegiance to him, describing 'the competition in Montinari's heart between Colli and Cantimori. In his heart only, because in his mind, Cantimori won' (144).

26 Montinari, 'Delio Cantimori e Nietzsche', *Su Nietzsche*, 108.

with Bertram's book, which shared themes with Mann's own politically conservative wartime screed *Observations of an Unpolitical Man* (1918) – a work in which 'Nietzsche's presence makes itself felt from the title to the last page' and whose influence can still be felt in Mann's *Doctor Faustus* (1947), albeit tempered by his interwar swing towards defending liberal democracy.[27] Montinari finds in Cantimori, as he does in Mann, a vector of deepening recognition of Nietzsche as a historical (rather than mythical) figure proceeding in tandem with his political shift from right to left.[28] His treatment of both men converges in his account of their understanding of Nietzsche's changing relationship to Wagner, which is also a major focus of *Che cosa ha detto Nietzsche*. Although he critiques the Cantimori of the 1930s for simplifying Nietzsche's work by failing to recognize the complexity of this relationship and hence implicitly subscribing to the construction – crucial to readings of Nietzsche that sought to keep him connected with Wagner's Germanic nationalism and antisemitism – of a basic continuity of Nietzsche's thought bridging their rupture, still he praises him for being able to distinguish between Nietzsche and such 'Nietzscheans' as Alfred Bäumler, Mussolini and Gabriele D'Annunzio.[29] By 1945 he sees Cantimori implicitly acknowledging the problem of 'deferred reading' by separating the fascist

27 Montinari, 'Lo scolaro di Goethe', *Su Nietzsche*, 67; translated as the Appendix to this volume, 155–64.

28 Cf. Giametta, *Colli, Montinari e Nietzsche*, 102–5, on Montinari's interest in Mann's swing to the left and on Mann as a model for Montinari's conception of the relationship between cultural work and political commitment.

29 'Without Nietzsche's own development, especially a sense of his break with Wagner and Schopenhauer, his theories have no internal history; but this . . . derives from the image of Nietzsche that Cantimori accepted, especially from Bertram.' Montinari, 'Delio Cantimori e Nietzsche', *Su Nietzsche*, 115–16.

Nietzsche from Nietzsche himself, and reports finally on a text of 1961 in which Cantimori asserts that 'Nietzsche forms part, and a capital part, of the real cultural history of Italy and Europe, and one must know him if one would know this reality, know him to understand it, seriously understand it, in order to make it progress and change.'[30] In a short essay of 1975, 'Goethe's Disciple: Notes on Nietzsche and Thomas Mann', translated in this volume, Montinari traces a comparable trajectory for Mann, from an early investment in Bertram's Nietzsche myth (1918), through a blunt rejection of Bäumler (1927) and the Nazi appropriation of Nietzsche, to the major reckoning of *Doctor Faustus* and of Mann's American lecture on 'Nietzsche's Philosophy in Light of Recent Experience' (both 1947), and beyond.[31] As with Cantimori, Montinari calls attention to Mann's assessment of Nietzsche's disrupted relationship to Wagner and Schopenhauer: 'in 1938 Thomas Mann – in his essay on the pessimistic philosopher – was able to say what many interpreters of Nietzsche have not sufficiently understood, when he defined the manner in which Nietzsche distanced himself from Wagner and Schopenhauer as "a great and decisive event in the history of the spirit"'.[32] At the same time, Montinari adds, 'Mann highlights the continuity of Nietzsche's development, noting Wagner's continuing presence up to the famous pages on *Tristan* in *Ecce Homo* and an "extension and transformation of the Schopenhauerian image of the world" in Nietzsche's philosophy.'[33] This assessment allows Montinari to

30 Ibid., 120–1.

31 See Appendix, 155–64.

32 Montinari, 'Lo scolaro di Goethe', *Su Nietzsche*, 70; this volume, 160. Montinari repeats this assessment nearly verbatim in *Che cosa ha detto Nietzsche*: 'Nietzsche's war against Wagner and the Wagnerian movement (and against antisemitism) is a capital fact in the history of German culture' (this volume, 75).

33 Montinari, 'Lo scolaro di Goethe', *Su Nietzsche*, 70; this volume, 161.

retain Nietzsche as a trenchant analyst, but not an advocate, of the kind of mythmaking the Nazis would later indulge in his name. Such calculations of continuities and ruptures in Nietzsche's development and in his reception by model disciples are Montinari's historical method of coming to terms with 'the richness and splendour, but also the misery, the disorientation, the sickness of *all* of Nietzsche', both as a thinker and as a set of events. If his work on the historical-critical edition was meant to enable the reader to stand freely face to face with this complex phenomenon, then *Che cosa ha detto Nietzsche* is both a means of reorientation and a guide to the forces of history that have obscured it from view.

Montinari's insistence on the intellectual discontinuity marked by Nietzsche's separation from Wagner and Schopenhauer is supported by his affection for the work he considered 'the first book that was really his': *Human, All Too Human* (1878–80).[34] For Montinari, this 'book for free spirits', dedicated to Voltaire in the year of the hundredth anniversary of his death, is an antimetaphysical work of Enlightenment, a rational organon for mental self-liberation, and (as he says in a somewhat defensive letter to Colli, whose tastes ran more to oracular texts like *Zarathustra*) 'the book that I feel I can endorse almost entirely'.[35] Conversely, his distaste for *Zarathustra* (1883–85) is palpable:

> The obsessive search for antitheses, the mode of expression overloaded with symbolism, the superabundance of similes

34 Montinari, 'Delio Cantimori e Nietzsche', *Su Nietzsche*, 108.

35 Letter of 22 August 1963, in Campioni, *Leggere Nietzsche*, 75 and 281. Cf. Colli, *Scritti su Nietzsche*, 109–23, on *Zarathustra*. Disputing Montinari's assessment of *Human, All Too Human* as an 'Enlightenment' text, Giametta critiques his preference for it as a way of attenuating discomfort with Nietzsche's more irrational and aggressive positions (*Colli, Montinari e Nietzsche*, 109–15).

> whose monotony derives from the way they nearly all repeat the same rhetorical patterns, the constant hammering of superlatives, Zarathustra's inability to 'warm the heart' of his readers, the total absence of joy despite Zarathustra's 'dancing' and 'laughter', the unchecked wordplay – all this makes *Thus Spoke Zarathustra* the grandiose antipode of a poetic work. It is a grotesque mistake to seek aesthetic pleasure in *Zarathustra*, just as it is to seek in it a substitute for religion or metaphysics.[36]

This is not simply a matter of style or temperament: *Zarathustra* had supposedly been the Nietzschean text most avidly read by German soldiers in the trenches of the First World War for its heroic bellicosity – a specially durable pocket edition of some 165,000 copies was produced for the purpose by Kröner in Leipzig – and it had been used in Entente propaganda to tar Germany with the brush of Nietzschean immoralism.[37] The Nazi deployment of *Zarathustra* in the Second World War was similar in kind (if perhaps not quite as extensive – Kröner seems to have focused instead on producing a volume of excerpts from Nietzsche, *Schwert des Geistes* [*Sword of the Spirit*], for soldierly use[38]) and focused especially (as Bäumler's jacket copy, again for Kröner, put it) on the idea of the *Übermensch* as 'the counter-image to Christian-democratic Europe' and on Nietzsche's doctrine of the

36 This volume, 103–4.

37 This despite the book's pan-European appeal throughout the first half of the twentieth century as a critique of decadence and a rousing glorification of war as culturally cathartic and regenerative. Cf. Aschheim, *The Nietzsche Legacy*, 132. Aschheim says 150,000 copies were printed; Hoffmann (*Zur Geschichte des Nietzsche-Archivs*, 88) says 165,000.

38 See Holub, 'The Elisabeth Legend', 215–16, on *Schwert des Geistes*, which he dates to 1941 but of which there are also editions of 1940 and 1944.

'eternal recurrence of the same', with its 'demand to do everything "in such a way that I would do it countless times"'.[39] Montinari pays special attention to how Nazi ideologues misunderstood these two key aspects of Nietzsche's thinking, their original discursive contexts, and the relationship between them.[40] By carefully establishing the natural philosopher Johannes Gustav Vogt, the revolutionary Louis-Auguste Blanqui and the polymath Gustave Le Bon as unrecognized historical interlocutors in Nietzsche's development of the idea of eternal recurrence, and by highlighting the concept's essential role in defining the *Übermensch*, Montinari is able to undermine the Nazi reification of the *Übermensch* as a racially superior type counterpointing eugenically eliminable *Untermenschen*.

> Nietzsche is not the overman; the overman is nothing other than the person who is able to say yes to life as it is, in eternal repetition. This is what links the theory of eternal recurrence with the doctrine of the overman. To accept total immanence, the world after the death of God, man must raise himself above himself, he must 'go under' so that the overman might be born . . . By keeping in mind, while reading *Zarathustra*, that the overman makes sense for Nietzsche *only* in relation to eternal recurrence, one can avoid gross misunderstandings and take both eternal recurrence and the overman for what they were in Nietzsche's mind: eternal recurrence is not a sort of *salto mortale* into irrationality in search of another 'world behind the world', or, worse, a bloodless surrogate for religion; the overman, precisely because of his connection with eternal recurrence, is not an aestheticizing athlete bursting

39 This text is not in the 1930 edition.

40 Cf. Campioni, *Leggere Nietzsche*, 185–96.

> with health or, worse yet, the prototype of a 'master race'. Rather, both are limiting concepts at the horizon of an anti-metaphysical and anti-pessimistic vision of the world, following the 'death of God'.[41]

For Montinari, *Zarathustra* is something of a watershed in Nietzsche's development. He evidently considers the early aphoristic volumes *Daybreak* (1881) and *The Gay Science* (1882) as more or less continuous with *Human, All Too Human*, but gives surprisingly short shrift to two major works, *Beyond Good and Evil* (1886) and *On the Genealogy of Morality* (1887), treating them alongside *Twilight of the Idols* (written 1888, published 1889), *The Antichrist* (written 1888, published 1895) and other late texts mostly as points in the arc of a longer development that failed to resolve itself into a *magnum opus*.[42] He has, however, a good deal to say about Nietzsche's final autobiographical text *Ecce Homo* (written 1888, published 1908), which he also refuses to consider finished. Here, again, we see him denying a text later used for mythical purposes its canonical status by drawing attention to the complex history of its composition. '*Ecce Homo* contains some of Nietzsche's most beautiful pages, and not only that: many key aspects of his personality first come to light in these pages. But *Ecce Homo* cannot be considered a "finished" text either, because Nietzsche continues to work on it up to the final day of his conscious life, adding parts and changing things even

41 This volume, 101–2. See also Campioni, *Leggere Nietzsche*, 190. Such insistence on the original discursive contexts of Nietzsche's thinking eventually led Montinari to attempt to reconstitute and catalogue Nietzsche's library, an effort completed by Campioni et al. in 2003. Giuliano Campioni, Paolo D'Iorio, Maria Cristina Fornari, Francesco Fronterotta, Andrea Orsucci and Renate Müller-Buck, eds., *Nietzsches persönliche Bibliothek* (Berlin: De Gruyter, 2003).

42 Cf. Giametta, *Colli, Montinari e Nietzsche*, 111.

after his revision of the manuscript at the beginning of December [1888]. This is why it is particularly important, while reading, to be aware of the order in which Nietzsche composed the various paragraphs'[43] – as well as of editorial suppressions such as that of the third paragraph of the chapter 'Why I Am So Wise', with its declaration, concerning 'the question of race', that the author is 'a pure-blooded Polish nobleman, without the admixture of a single drop of bad blood, least of all German', and the reflection that 'when I seek out the deepest contrast to myself, the incalculable baseness of instincts, what I always find is my mother and my sister – to believe myself to be related to such canaille would be a blasphemy against my divinity'.[44]

Colli and Montinari's project of publishing a new edition of Nietzsche began as a private undertaking. At its inception in 1961, only Colli was affiliated with a university (Pisa, where he taught history of ancient philosophy), and it would take them several difficult years to find publishers in Italy (Adelphi, 1964), France (Gallimard, 1965), Germany (De Gruyter, 1967) and Japan (Hakusuisha, 1979). Montinari's letters to Colli from Weimar between April 1961 and June 1970, usefully published in 1992 by Colli's student Giuliano Campioni, tell a fascinating story not only of Montinari's excited discoveries in the archive, of the two scholars' emotionally and intellectually complex relationship and of their developing thinking about the edition, but also of their interactions and negotiations with other scholars of Nietzsche, including the

43 This volume, 143.

44 Montinari, 'Ein neuer Abschnitt in Nietzsches "Ecce homo"', in *Nietzsche-Studien* 1 (1972): 380–418; translated as 'A New Section in Nietzsche's *Ecce Homo*' and 'Documentary Supplement', in Montinari, *Reading Nietzsche*, 103–40. Kaufmann omits this paragraph from his translation of 1967, which is perhaps not surprising, since the amended text was not published in the KGW until 1969.

archive's director, Karl-Heinz Hahn, scholars of the preceding generation such as Erich F. Podach and Karl Löwith, younger visitors to the archive such as Curt Paul Janz, Helmut Holtzhauer, Karl Pestalozzi and Walter Müller-Lauter, and Montinari's young assistants Sossio Giametta and Maria Ludovica Pampaloni, not to mention the archive employee who would become Montinari's wife and amanuensis in 1965, Sigrid Oloff. Hahn, Podach and Löwith would prove useful allies in their efforts, despite a break with Podach in 1963 that put paid to initial ideas about closer collaboration, while Pestalozzi and Müller-Lauter would step in as co-editors of the *Kritische Gesamtausgabe* upon Montinari's death in 1986. Montinari and Colli's first public presentation of their editorial enterprise occurs in July 1964, at the annual Royaumont Colloquium organized that year by the philosophers Martial Gueroult and Gilles Deleuze and attended by such established and emerging thinkers as Karl Löwith, Jean Wahl, Gianni Vattimo and Michel Foucault, an event now considered a seminal moment in the rediscovery and reinterpretation of Nietzsche's philosophy in France.[45] A letter to Colli of 13 May 1964 displays a concern with resistance to their approach, a fear that others might take the task out of their hands, and a desire to use the occasion to land a contract with a suitable German publisher:

> Above all, I would like to turn to the question of what tactics to adopt at Royaumont . . . I am of the opinion that we should not send in our talk in advance, but that we should just read it out, presenting it during the discussions on textual questions. It would be better if the others don't know what we want to say and are thus so to speak not immunized in advance, not warned and 'informed' about everything we have to say. In sum, it

45 Felsch, *How Nietzsche Came in From the Cold*, 1.

> seems important to me that *we* keep matters in our own hands, that we determine the theme of discussions of the edition.[46]

He had reason to worry: Nietzsche was still *persona non grata* in most of Europe, the two Italians were nearly completely unknown to the philosophical establishment (and to most participants in the symposium), and their historical-philological approach would prove to be sharply at odds with what the rising French poststructuralists would make of Nietzsche over the course of the 1960s and '70s. As Philipp Felsch has observed, Colli's assertion at Royaumont that 'he who interprets Nietzsche does him an injustice' and Montinari's recommendation of a moratorium on Nietzsche-interpretation until key philological problems were clarified were far apart from the deconstructive 'wild exegesis' to which Michel Foucault and Jacques Derrida would later subject Nietzsche's work. Nor was their approach amenable to the efforts of Gilles Deleuze or Jean-François Lyotard to 'actualize' Nietzsche for current culture-political purposes, the project announced in a second key French colloquium on Nietzsche in 1972 at Cerisy-la-Salle with the title 'Nietzsche aujourd'hui?', which Montinari and Colli did not attend.[47] Deleuze and Foucault's offer after Royaumont to co-edit the Gallimard edition of Nietzsche's works also predictably came to naught after the first volume, a translation of *The Gay Science*, was released in June 1967.[48]

The project's resonance was different in Italy and Germany. An unexpectedly popular fifteen-volume paperback critical study edition of Nietzsche's works and fragments by De Gruyter in 1980 would make its results widely available in German, while

46 Campioni, *Leggere Nietzsche*, 312–13.

47 Felsch, *How Nietzsche Came in From the Cold*, 1–12 and 145–51.

48 Ibid., 137–43.

Montinari's years of teaching at Urbino, Florence and Berlin (1971–81) and then of residency at the newly founded Wissenschaftskolleg in Berlin (1981–86), as well as his co-founding and editorship, with Walter Müller-Lauter, of the international journal *Nietzsche-Studien* in 1972, would consolidate his reputation as a leading authority on Nietzsche and as 'likely the only living person to have read every line left behind, every extant letter, in the original'.[49] His death of a sudden heart attack on 24 November 1986, the night before his inaugural lecture for a professorship at the University of Pisa, left a lacuna in Nietzsche scholarship that colleagues, students, friends and family have since filled with continuing philological and philosophical work, translations and biographical tributes, as well as critiques,[50] while Philipp Felsch's recent account of the editorial project, *How Nietzsche Came in from the Cold* (German 2023, English 2024), has excited public attention beyond the academy.

Che cosa ha detto Nietzsche, first published in 1975 by Ubaldini but acquired by Adelphi in 1999 and since then continuously in print, was translated into German for De Gruyter by Montinari's student Renate Müller-Buck in 1991 and reissued in 2003; there are also editions in Norwegian (1982), Greek (1998), French (2001) and Spanish (2003). Opining, in an early review, that Montinari's short book 'provides such a clear, sober, conscientiously balanced total picture that one would wish it the widest distribution', the American Germanist Reinhold Grimm called in 1976 for the text to be published in German and English.[51] I myself

49 Ibid., 7, quoting Frank Schirrmacher, literary editor of the *Frankfurter Allgemeine Zeitung*, shortly before Montinari's death in 1986.

50 Giametta and Felsch are notably critical voices.

51 Reinhold Grimm, '*Che cosa ha "veramente" detto Nietzsche*', *Monatshefte* 68.4 (1976): 448–50.

was inspired to translate the book into English by my first encounter some twenty years ago with Renate Müller-Buck's German translation of 1991, to which I would here acknowledge significant debt, both in the matter of finding solutions to problems of expression and for her work in finding the German originals of passages quoted from Nietzsche, not all of which Montinari identifies as such with quotation marks.[52] I have followed Müller-Buck in mostly restoring these marks and quoting Nietzsche verbatim, translating Montinari from the Italian and Nietzsche from the German while always endeavouring to adhere to the sense of Montinari's renderings into Italian. With some longer passages from Nietzsche's published works, I have reproduced the translations of widely available English-language editions, sometimes with modification. It is my hope that the reader will share my affection for the book's lucidity and sobriety, its concision, economy and balance, its intellectual honesty, and its judicious use of biography to illuminate the work, all of which clearly reflect the exceptional human – and humanistic – qualities of its author.

Peter J. Schwartz, Boston, 31 August 2025

52 Mazzino Montinari, *Friedrich Nietzsche: Eine Einführung*, trans. Renate Müller-Buck (Berlin: Walter De Gruyter, 1991). My translation follows Mazzino Montinari, *Che cosa ha detto Nietzsche*, edited and with a note by Giuliano Campioni (Milan: Adelphi, 1999).

Introduction

No philosopher's life has been explored in as much detail and from such a range of perspectives – for edification, in search of the 'scandal', of the key 'revelatory' event – as that of Friedrich Nietzsche. And, yet, some ninety years after the first Nietzsche biography, the state of affairs is not encouraging.[1] We know less about this life than ever, and every one of its phases confronts us with manifold questions that lack secure answers, especially where we are best supplied with biographical details. Nietzsche and Richard and Cosima Wagner, Nietzsche and Paul Rée and Lou Salomé, Nietzsche's illness, Nietzsche and his parents, Nietzsche and his friends: these are the classic themes the biographers have felt compelled to address, whether treating the whole of Nietzsche's life or only parts of it. With scant success, as we have noted: They have almost invariably exaggerated data that had been laboriously assembled or ingeniously intuited, and which was thus all the more overvalued.

Besides the works that Nietzsche himself published during his conscious lifetime (or left 'print-ready'), there is an imposing mass of notebooks, files and loose manuscript pages whose partial and unscholarly publication by the former Nietzsche-Archive in

1 Ola Hansson, *Friedrich Nietzsche: Seine Persönlichkeit und sein System* (Leipzig: Fritzsch, 1890). [Some ninety years, reckoning backward from Montinari's date of publication (1975). Trans.]

Weimar (1894–1945) has produced its own sort of confusion with regard to the subject that drives scholars to concern themselves *also* with Nietzsche's biography: his thought. The primary documents for any biography – that is to say, the letters – were published still more imperfectly and incompletely than the manuscripts. This is a serious lacuna, hardly to be remedied with the 'leaked' epistolary texts copied in secret by the first editor of Nietzsche's works, Fritz Kögel,[2] during the years of his short but extremely intense activity in the employ of the founder of the Nietzsche Archive and the Nietzsche 'cult': the philosopher's sister, Elisabeth Förster-Nietzsche (1846–1935). It is impossible to say if the 'historical-critical' edition of Nietzsche's works and letters, interrupted by the war (1933–42: five volumes of the published works, four volumes of the letters), would really have represented the 'liberating act' promised by one of its editors, the classical philologist Hans Joachim Mette.[3] In any case, this promise, made in a brochure of 1932 announcing the new critical edition, was omitted from the final text of the introduction to the works published in the first volume. There are texts in Nietzsche's literary estate that the Nazi canaille who ultimately controlled the destiny of the Nietzsche-Archive would hardly have approved of.

In any event, an entirely new situation developed in the field of Nietzsche studies when the Goethe and Schiller Archive in Weimar, in the German Democratic Republic, opened up all the collections of the former Nietzsche-Archive to researchers, leading to a boom in Nietzsche studies over roughly the last twenty

2 David Marc Hoffmann, 'Die Kogel-Exzerpte', *Zur Geschichte des Nietzsche-Archivs* (Berlin: De Gruyter, 1991), 579–713.

3 Hans Joachim Mette, *Der handschriftliche Nachlass Friedrich Nietzsches* (Leipzig: Hadl, 1932), 82.

years.[4] This has produced significant new results with regard to both the biography and the texts. While the 'objective' difficulties with writing Nietzsche's biography are thus disappearing, we must add that writing a history of Nietzsche's life requires us to base the clarification of biographical details, the retrieval of unknown texts and the correction of certain falsifications upon the methodological premise (which holds not only for Nietzsche's biography) that any attempt to establish a causal relationship between Nietzsche's life events and his thought is doomed to failure. One almost has the impression that our sense of Nietzsche becomes more elusive whenever new biographical data come to light. This elusiveness can be explained only if we address the question of what Nietzsche's life really is. Nietzsche's life consists of his thoughts, of his books. Nietzsche is a rare example of mental concentration, of a cruel and continuous exercise of the intellect, of the interiorization and sublimation of personal experiences, from the most dramatic to the most insignificant. He exemplifies the reduction of what is commonly called 'life' to 'spirit', meant in the sense of the German word *Geist*, that is to say: mind–reason–intellect, understood also as interiority or spirituality (but not in the mystical sense of *Seele* or anima). What then is spirit, what is *Geist* for Nietzsche? 'Spirit is life that itself cuts into life; by its own agony it increases its own knowledge . . . You know only the spark of the spirit, but you do not see the anvil that it is, nor the cruelty of its hammer!'[5] Provided we never forget this essential characteristic of Nietzsche's, research on the

4 [Again, dating backward from 1975. Trans.]

5 *Thus Spoke Zarathustra: A Book for All and None*, edited by Adrian Del Caro and Robert Pippin, translated by Adrian Del Caro (Cambridge: Cambridge University Press, 2006), Second Part, 'On the Famous Wise Men', 80.

biographical particulars can avoid the temptation of focusing on them too narrowly and overvaluing them on account of the effort expended in collecting them. It can thus become meaningful, and it must, in any case, be radical and 'merciless'. Thus, we can also perceive how, for Nietzsche, every thought was an event, every book that he published an 'overcoming'. Nietzsche wrote for himself; for him, to write was to live. This much can be gathered from his intimate notebooks, which – with some minor exceptions, a matter of a few dozen pages from among thousands – are dedicated to the continuous and 'expressive' registration of philosophical meditations, psychological intuitions, moral observations, often already cast in the form in which they would be published, and whose external occasion is difficult to reconstruct. Their subject, meanwhile, is not Nietzsche himself, at least not in the sense in which Stendhal, in his diaries, could be the subject of his own introspection.

These notebooks are a record of interiorized events that have already been mediated – filtered through the medium of expression, through writing. We do not know the anvil from which the sparks of Nietzsche's aphorisms flew, and we gain some sense of the cruelty of the hammer from the lucid and perfect 'cruelty' of the formulation.

In order to become himself in this way, Nietzsche severed one after another all the bonds that connected him with ordinary life; at least, he attempted to reduce them to a minimum, ending as the celebrant of a 'life' that was ever less 'life', ever more 'spirit'.

1
Nietzsche's Childhood and Youth (1844–69)

1. 'The village of Röcken stretches along the provincial road that leads from Weißenfels to Lützen. It is enclosed by willow thickets and scattered poplars and elms, so that from a distance only the jutting chimneys and the old-fashioned church tower are visible through the green treetops. The village includes a number of fair-sized ponds, separated by thin strips of land; it is green all around, with knobbly willows. The pastor's house and the church are set somewhat higher up, the former surrounded by gardens and plantings of trees. The cemetery is close by, full of sunken gravestones and crosses. The rectory itself stands in the shadow of three majestic, broad-boughed acacias.'[1] Thus did the fifteen-year-old Nietzsche, in one of his many autobiographical sketches, describe the village of Röcken, located (after 1815) in Prussian Saxony, where he was born on 15 October 1844.

The 'pastor's house', the cemetery, the ponds, but, above all, the pastor of the small Lutheran community of Röcken, that is to say his father Carl Ludwig Nietzsche, dominate his childhood memories. 'As a plant I was born near the cemetery, as a man, in

1 Friedrich Nietzsche, *Nachgelassene Aufzeichnungen. Herbst 1862–Sommer 1864*, ed. Johann Figl and Hans Gerald Hodl (Berlin: Walter De Gruyter, 2006), 190-91 (*Kritische Gesamtausgabe* [KGW], I.3).

the pastor's house' is how Nietzsche put it at age nineteen.[2] 'He was delicate, kind and sickly, as if destined for only a fleeting appearance in this world': this is the portrait that Nietzsche paints of his father – dead at thirty-six, when the boy was not yet five years old – in *Ecce Homo*, the last and best known of his autobiographies (1888).[3]

From his father, Nietzsche inherited his passion for music, his religious sense of duty, his alacrity and diligence in work, his force of will, but also an easily excitable nervous system, prone to states of depression and exaltation. The serious migraines that Nietzsche suffered from starting in late adolescence were probably also a paternal legacy.

As the young Nietzsche relates and all other sources attest without exception, Carl Ludwig Nietzsche died of a brain disease; inflammation of the brain with consequent 'cerebral softening' was the doctor's diagnosis, in the vague terminology of the period. It may well have been a tumour.

'In September 1848', writes Nietzsche, not yet fourteen, 'my beloved father suddenly contracted a mental illness.'[4] Elisabeth Förster-Nietzsche, publishing this sentence of her brother's for the first time, falsified it as follows: 'In September 1848, my beloved father suddenly became gravely ill as a result of a fall.'[5] Förster-Nietzsche thus harmonized her brother's view of their father's malady with her own, given a few pages earlier in the first

---

2 Ibid., 190.

3 *Ecce Homo*, 'Why I Am So Wise', 1.

4 Friedrich Nietzsche, *Werke und Briefe. Historisch-kritische Gesamtausgabe*, ed. Hans Joachim Mette, Karl Schlechta and Carl Koch (Munich: Beck, 1933–40; reprint, Munich: Deutscher Taschenbuch Verlag, 1994), vol. 1, 4 [hereinafter BAW].

5 Elisabeth Förster-Nietzsche, *Das Leben Friedrich Nietzsche's*, vol. I (Leipzig: Naumann, 1895), 19.

volume of her biography of Nietzsche, published in 1895: 'One evening toward the end of August 1848, he [Carl Ludwig Nietzsche] walked some friends home; on his return, our little dog ran between his legs at the doorsill of the parish house – he tripped and fell backwards down seven stone steps, onto the pavement of the courtyard. This caused a concussion; his health began to fail, and he died 11 months afterward.'[6] What led the sister to introduce this falsification was the danger that the general theories of heredity widespread in the nineteenth century might allow a link to be made between the father's 'nervous illness' and Nietzsche's. To head off the question of heredity, Elisabeth Förster-Nietzsche had to promote the idea of a traumatic rather than an organic origin of their father's illness.

Naturally, the sources from the time of Carl Ludwig's illness include no evidence of his falling down the steps. Of particular importance in this regard are the letters that the philosopher's mother, Franziska Nietzsche, wrote during this period (October 1848–September 1849) to a pair of family friends, the archdeacon Emil Julius Schenk and his wife Emma in Zeitz, to keep them apprised of the progress of her husband's malady. Here, she describes the symptoms of the illness: headaches, vomiting, paralytic symptoms in the hands and tongue, dizziness. And it is the same Franziska Nietzsche, fearing the unknown disease that had stricken her husband, who naively advances the hypothesis of a hereditary illness: she speaks in fact of a family destiny, of the father's inherited malady, in a letter of 16 October 1848.

Nietzsche himself suffered throughout his life (especially after 1873) from attacks of headache and vomiting lasting up to three days at a time, but, while it is possible that the migraines that tortured him were inherited from his father, it cannot be said for

6 Ibid., 5.

certain that there was a connection between these migraines and his father's brain disease, however similar they may appear, just as it is impossible to establish a link between Nietzsche's *final* illness and the one that killed his father. When, however, his migraine attacks reached their apex, in 1879, Nietzsche thought he would die in the same way his father did.

Elisabeth Förster-Nietzsche takes to the field against this tendency of her relatives, of mother and brother, to seek hereditary taints in the family. She does so as early as 1889, when she learns of her brother's illness, and, writing from Paraguay, disapproves of her poor mother Franziska for having dared to advance the novel hypothesis of a family malady to explain her son's dementia. We thus already find in this letter to her mother Förster-Nietzsche's ridiculous thesis that Nietzsche's collapse in Turin in January 1889 had been brought on by an abuse of sleeping pills. Some years later, in 1895, in the first volume of her biography of her brother, she takes pains to demonstrate that all of Nietzsche's ascendants and more or less distant relatives, on both sides of the family, had been robust and long-lived and – above all – 'of sound mind'.[7] Förster-Nietzsche's line makes sense when we consider that, besides the understandable desire to defend the 'good name' of the family and of her brother, she harboured the fear that Nietzsche's philosophy itself might be compromised if it were possible to demonstrate the existence of a hereditary taint. And, in fact, there are plenty of attempts at 'psychopathology' in the Nietzsche literature that endeavour to explain his thought by his illness (hereditary or not).

It is almost amusing to watch, on the one hand, the Nietzsche devotees (his sister at their head) straining to demonstrate Nietzsche's 'congenital' health, and, on the other, the doctors or

7 Ibid., 10 and 13.

so-called psychiatrists with philosophical ambitions attempting to exorcize an unpleasant and dangerous philosophy by extrapolating from a hereditary pathology in Nietzsche to his thinking. Both parties are victims of a positivistic prejudice: that is, of the idea that by virtue of being the product of a so-called diseased (but sane) mind, this philosophy is itself diseased (albeit sane). This is not to say that illness as a lived experience, including Nietzsche's experience of his father's malady, was not important to his life and philosophy: we need only think of the reflections on illness that recur constantly in his works and letters. It is, however, ridiculous to pull out the easy excuse that we must be on guard against what he wrote because his books are the product of a sick brain.[8]

From the research of Richard Blunck, the most recent and indeed the best biographer of Nietzsche's childhood, we learn that Nietzsche's father suffered from epileptic attacks, starting before, and independent of, his fatal illness.[9] Nietzsche, too, declared to the doctors at the asylum in Jena on 5 September 1889 that he had suffered from 'epileptic states without loss of consciousness, up to the age of seventeen'.[10] The lack of contemporary testimony regarding epileptic attacks in the young Nietzsche (by teachers, for example) does not suffice to disqualify this declaration on the subject by the mad Nietzsche himself. Contemporary testimony shows that, during the first years of his malady, he had in fact an exact idea of his own past. The interest that Nietzsche shows in his works (for example *Daybreak*,

8 Paul Julius Möbius, *Nietzsche. Ausgewählte Werke*, vol. V (Leipzig: Barth, 1904), 194.

9 Richard Blunck, *Friedrich Nietzsche. Kindheit und Jugend* (Munich: Ernst Reinhardt Verlag, 1953).

10 Jena clinical files, in Pia Daniela Volz, *Nietzsche im Labyrinth seiner Krankheit. Eine medizinisch-biographische Untersuchung* (Würzburg: Konigshausen & Neumann, 1990), 404.

aphorism 87) in the problem of 'masked epilepsy' when he attempts to explain certain phenomena of the religious life could be considered indirect evidence that he was speaking of such phenomena based on personal experience. But this is something we can only suppose. Meanwhile, we can do no more than suggest a possible parallel between Nietzsche's life and his father's. Epilepsy is, in fact, not hereditary (in the sense that Carl Ludwig Nietzsche could have transmitted it to his son; it could however have been congenital; that is, Nietzsche could have contracted it in his mother's womb). A psychoanalyst might hypothesize a sort of unconscious imitation by Nietzsche of his father's fate. What is certain is that the illness and premature death of his father were constantly present in Nietzsche's memory, from childhood through his adult years.

While we are speaking of Nietzsche's father, we must not fail to mention two posthumous fragments, from 1875 and 1878 respectively, the only ones written by the adult Nietzsche on the subject of his dead father. These were published in the first edition of Nietzsche's works,[11] but then suppressed in all subsequent editions by Förster-Nietzsche, perhaps because she believed that they could be interpreted in a pathological sense (as hallucinations, for example, to use terminology the present author has only recently discovered to be unsound).[12] In these fragments, Nietzsche writes: 'in the Neugasse, where I always heard the admonishing voice of my

11 Friedrich Nietzsche, *Werke*, ed. Fritz Kögel, 12 vols (Leipzig: Naumann, 1895–97).

12 Thanks to the clarifications of my medical and 'anti-psychiatric' friend Giorgio Antonucci, who has induced me to revise thoroughly this entire segment of my work; cf. however M. Montinari, *Nietzsche*, 'I Protagonisti della Storia Universale', vol. XI (Milan: CEI, 1968), 284.

father',[13] and '*Daimonion* – admonishing voice of my father'.[14] The Neugasse is the street Nietzsche lived on in Naumburg shortly after having left Röcken, from April 1850 to May 1856, thus from age six to age twelve. The two fragments testify to an intimate and secret bond, beginning in childhood, between Nietzsche and his dead father. For him, the relationship with his father signified, above all, a relationship with the religion of the fathers, and also with illness, with 'decadence', as Nietzsche says

---

13 *Nachgelassene Fragmente* (posthumous fragments) [hereinafter NF]: NF 11[11], 1875. [The *Nachgelassene Fragmente* are now all available in German in Friedrich Nietzsche, *Werke. Kritische Gesamtausgabe* (hereinafter KGW), founding editors Giorgio Colli and Mazzino Montinari, continued by Volker Gerhardt, Norbert Miller, Wolfgang Müller-Lauter and Karl Pestalozzi (Berlin: Walter de Gruyter, 1967–); some are reproduced in selected volumes of the English translation of Nietzsche's works published by Stanford University Press. Because providing page references would unduly swell these footnotes, I have chosen to adhere to Colli and Montinari's standard numbering system, which organizes the posthumous material by dated and archivally numbered notebooks or looseleaf manuscript groups. NF 28(9), 1878, for example, designates the ninth fragment in notebook twenty-eight of the year 1878. Likewise, I have not provided page references for Nietzsche's correspondence, which is available in German in Nietzsche, *Briefwechsel. Kritische Gesamtausgabe*, founding editors Giorgio Colli and Mazzino Montinari, continued by Norbert Miller and Annemarie Pieper (Berlin: Walter de Gruyter, 1974–2004), or in the extensive selection in Nietzsche, *Sämtliche Briefe. Kritische Studienausgabe*, ed. Giorgio Colli and Mazzino Montinari (Berlin: Walter de Gruyter, 1986). The complete posthumous fragments and correspondence are both available online at nietzschesource.org/#eKGWB. When citing Nietzsche's published works, I have only provided page numbers to English translations when I have made significant use of them in the text. Nietzsche's predilection for aphorisms and short numbered chapters should make cited passages easy to find, both in the original German and in all available translations. Trans.]

14 NF 28[9], 1878.

in *Ecce Homo*.[15] It also meant the solitude in which this 'admonishing voice' could reach him.

2. 'I am solitude become man . . .' – this is how Nietzsche defined himself a few days before madness removed him from every conscious contact with the world.[16] 'At an absurdly early age, at seven, I already knew that no human word would ever reach me', Nietzsche writes in *Ecce Homo*,[17] immediately counterbalancing this melancholy statement with the sinister euphoria of the impending catastrophe: 'has anyone ever seen me saddened on this account?' Up to the present day, no one has been able to establish the significance of Nietzsche's assertion that he traced his sense of being alone to the 'absurd age' of seven. We know that this refers to a real childhood episode, already recorded in two mutually illuminating autobiographical notes written in 1875 and 1878, thus thirteen and ten years prior to *Ecce Homo* and to Nietzsche's loss of sanity: 'at Pobles, when I cried over my lost childhood'; 'At seven years – feeling of the loss of childhood'.[18] As he often reports in his early autobiographical texts, the young Nietzsche enjoyed many happy vacations at Pobles, another village in Saxony, home to his maternal grandfather David Ernst Oehler, also a Protestant pastor. However, we find not a single word in these texts concerning a 'loss of childhood' experienced at the age of seven, although they include detailed memories of many other events. This reserve on the subject, even to himself, increases the value of the testimonies of 1875, 1878 and 1888. These notes of 1875 and, especially, those of 1878 are not isolated,

15 *Ecce Homo*, 'Why I Am So Wise', 1.

16 NF 25[7], 1888–89.

17 *Ecce Homo*, 'Why I Am So Clever', 10.

18 NF 11[11], 1875; NF 28[8], 1878.

but are rather accompanied by other reminiscences of childhood, finally finding a damped (and, as always, depersonalized) echo in aphorism 168 of *The Wanderer and His Shadow*: 'the bliss of childhood and the loss of childhood, the sense of that which is irretrievable, as of the most precious possession . . .'

Our image of Nietzsche's life between the ages of seven and fifteen is considerably changed by this, not only with respect to his sister's stories, but also with regard to the writings of the young Nietzsche (at least those that have come down to us and of which we are aware, since we cannot exclude the possibility that Förster-Nietzsche destroyed any that may have seemed to her to compromise her brother's 'good name'). Yet there is no need to one-sidedly view Nietzsche's entire childhood in the light of precocious solitude and a secret rapport with his father and with disease. Nietzsche took part in the games of his classmates, and he both loved and practised at least two sports: ice skating – there were two ponds near Naumburg on which he skated with friends in the winter – and swimming. He was already an indefatigable walker, and the excursions he took to numerous castles on the banks of the Saale were memorable events for him. In sum, Nietzsche was *also* a normal boy. There are no outward traces of the second life that we have barely intuited here, perhaps aside from the observation by relatives, friends and teachers that the young Nietzsche seemed 'to have been made for solitude' – a fact that was never a cause for concern.[19] The caesura at the age of seven – the 'loss of childhood' – thus remains little more than a hint at some subterranean evolution.

After the death of Carl Ludwig Nietzsche, in 1850, the family of the young Friedrich, comprised of his mother, little Elisabeth (born

19 Wilhelm Pinder, cited in Förster-Nietzsche, *Das Leben Friedrich Nietzsche's*, 31–2.

in 1846), Nietzsche's paternal grandmother and two aunts, also from the father's side of the family, moved to the quiet city of Naumburg. The education given the two siblings by the young widow – Franziska Nietzsche, née Oehler – helped by the other women in the home and by numerous relatives, nearly all of them Protestant pastors, was rigorously and, on the whole, naively Protestant. Like her son, Franziska had a violent and impetuous temperament. Her profoundly healthy nature was quite the opposite of the 'morbidity' of her dead husband, her belief was free from all doubts, her faith in God unshakable. She constantly tried to keep her son from being 'different from the others' and from spending all his time reading, writing poetry and making music; to her Nietzsche owed his inclination to healthy living and physical exercise.

We cannot doubt the profound impression that these years of religious education made upon Nietzsche. 'As a child, I saw God in his glory', writes the author of *Human, All Too Human* in a personal note.[20] It is true that he would add soon thereafter: 'As a relative of Protestant pastors, I quickly understood their intellectual and psychological limitations', but also 'their industry, pride, sense of decorum'.[21] The young Nietzsche was doubtless bound to rebel soon enough; but this reaction was born from the ground of familial piety. Nietzsche also seems to allude to a subtle nexus between freethinking and his environment, which was that of Lutheran religiosity, in a famous aphorism (324) from the *Assorted Opinions and Maxims* (1879): 'The most dangerous region in Germany is Saxony and Thüringen [where Nietzsche was born and raised]: nowhere is there more spiritual agility and knowledge of humanity, as well as free-spiritedness, and all of it is so modestly concealed by the hideous language and the zealous servility of the

20 NF 28[7], 1878.

21 Ibid.

population, that we hardly notice that we are dealing with spiritual sergeants of Germany and its schoolmasters in good and bad.'[22] In fact, what we see in that short autobiographical note about seeing God in his glory is a trace of Nietzsche's own earliest freethinking: 'First philosophical writing about the origin of the Devil (God thinks himself, he can only do this by imagining his opposite).'[23] In his preface to *On the Genealogy of Morality* (1887), Nietzsche says that he wrote this 'first philosophical exercise' – now apparently lost – at the age of thirteen.

The young Nietzsche's education was thus dominated by a religiosity whose centre was the individual's direct relationship with God, and which – precisely for this reason – guided a person toward continuous meditation upon God, Nature and human beings. What is more, as Delio Cantimori has observed of the influence of Martin Luther, in the families of Protestant pastors people not only assiduously read the Bible, but also loved poetry and, above all, music and song.[24] The memory of melodies first heard in childhood is the principal theme of the aphorism in which Nietzsche speaks of 'lost childhood'. In his reminiscences, Nietzsche frequently mentions the 'Evening Song' of Matthias Claudius – still one of the most popular and well-known *Lieder* for any German child today – not only in his youthful writings, but also in 1875, when, interrupting the difficult drafting of his *Unfashionable Observation* on Richard Wagner, he abandons himself to reminiscing upon the happy days in his life. Nor would

22 *Human, All Too Human II and Unpublished Fragments from the Period of Human, All Too Human II (Spring 1878–Fall 1879)*, trans. Gary Handwerk (Stanford, CA: Stanford University Press, 2013), 126–7.

23 NF 28[7], 1878, 126–7.

24 Delio Cantimori, *Lutero*, 'I Protagonisti della Storia Universale', vol. V (Rome-Milan: CEI, 1966), 533–60.

the grown man ever forget that day in his youth when his paternal grandfather explained to him the poem 'Country Life', by the late-eighteenth-century sentimental poet Ludwig Christian Hölty.[25] Handel's *Messiah* and *Judas Maccabeus*, the *Creation* of Haydn, Mozart's *Requiem*, and the works of Beethoven and Bach, Schubert and Mendelssohn (in particular, the *Midsummer Night's Dream*) fascinated and deeply moved the young Nietzsche, who resolved to compose music himself, and generally developed 'an undying hatred for all modern music and for anything that was not classical'.[26] Liszt, Berlioz and Wagner were what were understood at the time as modern music, or 'the music of the future'.

In Nietzsche's, as in all Protestant families, the religious festivals and family anniversaries were occasions not only for rest from daily work, but also for dedicating oneself to music and poetry. For the young Nietzsche, the birthdays of relatives, especially those of his mother and paternal grandfather, were occasions for presenting the fruits of his poetic and musical labours: he began writing poetry at eight and composing music at eleven. But none of Nietzsche's pious relatives could possibly have imagined what fruits would be borne by this plant grown from the humus of such an 'interiority protected by power' (*machtgeschützte Innerlichkeit*, Thomas Mann), out of the typical Lutheran *Gemütlichkeit*.

3. Nietzsche began to reflect methodically on himself, and to write down these reflections, around the age of twelve. We can count about a dozen attempts at autobiography between 1856 and 1863, besides diaries written during vacations or occasioned by short journeys and other events, in which he always attempts to analyse his 'mood'.

---

25 NF 11[11], 1875.

26 BAW I, 18.

'On Moods' (*Über Stimmungen*) is also the title of an essay written at the age of nineteen, probably under the influence of Emerson's *Essays* (1858), a book that Nietzsche would read and reread throughout the course of his life. 'Let us confess it, I am writing about moods, while currently being in a mood; and it is fortunate that I am precisely in the mood to describe moods.' Moods are like guests of our souls, 'but it is strange', he continues: 'the guests do not come because we want them to, and they do not come as they are; rather, the ones that come do so because they must, and only the ones who must, come. Whatever the soul cannot reflect does not affect it; but because it is in the power of the will to make the soul reflect or not, only what the soul wants to affect it can do so . . . One of the soul's strongest inclinations is however a certain curiosity, a propensity for the unusual, and this explains why we often put ourselves into disquieting moods.'[27] This passage exemplifies the absolute lack of immediacy, the 'cerebral' nature, of Nietzsche's writings, which were yet all born of 'moods', often disturbing ones. Before sensing the 'pathos of distance' in others, Nietzsche first sensed it in himself. He constantly endeavours to give a style not only to thoughts, but to the soul. This proceeds from a constant tension of the mind, of the 'spirit', which is why it is pointless to seek 'poetry' in either the conventional compositions of his youth or the dithyrambs of the late Nietzsche. Everything in him was 'reflected' – both the pain and the ecstasy. This helps us better to understand the ambivalence inherent in Nietzsche's valuation of poetic creativity, and of artistic creativity in general.

The fascination that Nietzsche felt with regard to anything that might help him to analyse himself is also expressed in the following lines, written at the age of fifteen on reading Laurence Sterne,

---

27 BAW II, 406–7.

in 1859: '*Tristram Shandy* . . . attracts me immensely; I am taking notes for myself on all the ideas that strike me. Never before have I encountered such a dissection of the heart.'[28] Let us note, in passing, that Förster-Nietzsche transformed these extracts from *Tristram Shandy* into so many original philosophical maxims by the young Nietzsche himself.[29] Recalling the death of his paternal grandmother, which had occurred in April 1856, Nietzsche, barely fourteen, observed: 'It is a singular characteristic of the human heart that if we have experienced a great loss, we do not try to forget it, but rather recall it to mind as often as we can. It is as if we truly drew solace for our pain from the repeated narration.'[30] For Nietzsche, 'moods' were never an end in themselves.

It was in Naumburg that Nietzsche met the two greatest friends of his life. One of them, Gustav Krug, was the son of a magistrate who was an amateur composer and had friendly relations with Felix Mendelssohn. Gustav played the violin and introduced Nietzsche to the music of Wagner (in 1861, with a piano transcription of *Tristan*, which Nietzsche would recall in a famous passage of *Ecce Homo*).[31] If Gustav represented one of Nietzsche's predilections – for music – the other friend, Wilhelm Pinder, also a magistrate's son, shared his passion for poetry.

One day, 25 July 1860 – Nietzsche was already a student at Pforta – the three friends arranged to meet in the ruins of a castle near Naumburg, where with a solemn ceremony, and swearing an oath, they founded an association that they dubbed 'Germania'. Alluding to this episode in 1872, Nietzsche recalled: 'We decided then to found a little association of a few comrades, with the aim

---

28 BAW I, 151.

29 Förster-Nietzsche, *Das Leben Friedrich Nietzsche's*, 130–1.

30 BAW I, 21.

31 *Ecce Homo*, 'Why I Am So Clever', 6.

of establishing a solid and binding organization for our productive inclinations in art and literature. To put it more simply: we each committed ourselves to delivering, from month to month, a product of our own, be it a poetic work or an essay or an architectural sketch or a musical composition, and each of the others had a right to judge this product with the unlimited frankness of friendly critique. We thought this mutual surveillance a good way both to stimulate and to control our drive to improve our minds.'[32] 'Germania' lasted three years, and for it Nietzsche composed music, wrote poetry and gave lectures of a philosophical, historical and literary character. Among the themes he broached for his association we find, to begin, the saga of the Ostrogothic king Ermanarich,[33] who inspired in him several dramatic projects as well as the idea of composing a symphonic poem. It is worth noting the sixteen-year-old Nietzsche's judgement upon these efforts: 'my characters lack the powerful character traits and qualities of the ancient Germans; the feelings are rather tortured, modernized – too much reflection and too little natural force'.[34] What seems significant here, even more than the anticipation of Nietzsche's encounter and subsequent break with the world of Wagner's Nibelungen that Blunck perceives in these lines, is the record of Nietzsche's futile struggle to break through to nature and to 'poetry' by transcending 'reflection'.[35]

4. In 1858, Nietzsche had left his family to finish secondary school at the venerable Pforta school, located an hour's walk from

32 'Über die Zukunft unserer Bildungsanstalten. Erster Vortrag' (On the Future of Our Educational Institutions. First Lecture), KGW III/2, 145–6.

33 BAW I, 290–9.

34 BAW II, 101.

35 Blunck, *Friedrich Nietzsche*, 73.

Naumburg.[36] Many illustrious alumni had studied at Pforta, founded in the sixteenth century, including Klopstock, Johann Elias Schlegel, Fichte and Ranke. The school enjoyed great prestige for its educational system, for its simple and healthy way of life – physical exercise was not neglected – and for the high quality of its teachers.

The six years at Pforta were a decisive factor in Nietzsche's formation. The rigorous daily schedule, the quasi-military organization, the challenging curricula were, for Nietzsche, a healthy disciplinary regime within which his strong and nearly chaotic impulses, his disorderly thirst for knowledge, could be both 'stimulated and controlled'.[37] On the other hand, it was precisely 'this almost military compulsion, which, designed to have an effect on the mass, deliberately treats the individual in a cold, superficial way, that guided me back to myself. I salvaged my private inclinations and aspirations from the uniform law.'[38] In the spirit of Pforta and on the basis of personal experience, Nietzsche would write as late as 1888:

> I cannot see how one can make up for not having attended a *good school* at the right time. Such a person does not know himself; he walks through life without having learned to walk; the weak musculature reveals itself at every step . . . Invariably, the most desirable thing is a hard discipline *at the right time*: that is, to see much demanded of one at the moment in life when this fills one with pride. For this is what distinguishes the hard school, as a good school, from all others: that it demands a great deal, and demands it inflexibly; that the good, that even the excellent is

36 *Ecce Homo*, 'Why I Am So Clever', 1.

37 'Über die Zukunft unserer Bildungsanstalten. Erster Vortrag' (On the Future of Our Educational Institutions. First Lecture), KGW III/2, 145–6.

38 BAW V, 252.

> expected as something normal; that censure is expressed sharply, objectively, and without regard to talent or social origins.[39]

Mastery of the historical-critical method in reading texts, a direct and extensive knowledge of the most important authors of Greek and Latin antiquity, an assiduous perfection of style for which Nietzsche took Sallust as a model, are all products of these six years. Nietzsche's drifting away from the religion of the fathers can also be traced to this period.

Among the modern authors whose names recur most frequently in the essays and letters of this period we find Emerson, Sterne, Byron, Schiller, Goethe, Hölderlin, Novalis, Kerner, Platen and Cervantes, as well as Alexander von Humboldt, Ludwig Feuerbach (*The Essence of Christianity*), Hermann Hettner's *Literary History of the Eighteenth Century* (1856–70), and historiographical works such as Eduard Arnd's *History of the French Revolution* (1851). We also encounter the names of two popular authors, now forgotten: Franz Gaudy and Ludwig Rellstab.

An essay written for 'Germania' is dedicated to the dramatic compositions of Byron (*Sardanapalus*, *Marino Faliero*, *The Two Foscari*, but above all *Manfred*), an old and enduring love of Nietzsche's.[40] 'A deep affinity linked me to Byron's *Manfred*', he would write in *Ecce Homo*. 'All these abysses I found in myself; at the age of thirteen I was ripe for this work.'[41] *Manfred*'s 'abysses' seem also to have opened in the emotion registered by the fifteen-year-old on rereading Schiller's *Robbers*: 'Yesterday I reread *The Robbers*', he writes in one of his journals at Pforta, on 24 August 1859. 'Each time I read this play I experience a strange sensation.

39 NF 14[161], 1888.

40 BAW I, 9–15.

41 *Ecce Homo*, 'Why I Am So Clever', 4.

To me the characters appear nearly superhuman, they seem to participate in a titanic struggle against religion and virtue in which however the celestial omnipotence achieves an infinitely tragic victory. Terrible in the end is the despair of the infinite sinner [*des unendlichen Sünders*], which is increased horrifically by the words of the father.'[42] The titanic evil of Schiller's thoroughly contemptible 'infinite sinner' Franz Moor seems psychologically very close to the titanic and darkly desperate evil of Byron's Manfred. But Nietzsche's favourite poet was Hölderlin, practically unknown at the time, all of whose then-published poetry he read with emotion, as well as the dramatic fragment *The Death of Empedocles* and the novel *Hyperion*. In a school composition of 19 October 1861, Nietzsche declares this predilection and defends Hölderlin against prejudices then widespread even among specialists, who saw in the unhappy Swabian poet little more than 'a curiosity of German literature'.[43] In the melancholy tones of the *Empedocles* Nietzsche senses 'the future of the unfortunate poet, the sepulchre of his long years of insanity', not in the form of obscure ramblings, 'but rather in the purest Sophoclean language and in an infinite plenitude of profound thoughts'.[44] The death of Empedocles 'is a death from divine pride, from contempt for humanity, from a satiation with life on earth and from pantheism. Reading this work has always affected me particularly: there is a divine majesty in this Empedocles.'[45] The judgement of his teacher at Pforta, the Germanist Koberstein, was: 'I must impart to the author the friendly advice that he turn his attentions to a healthier, clearer, *more German* poet.'[46]

42 BAW I, 137.

43 Blunck, *Friedrich Nietzsche*, 59.

44 BAW II, 2.

45 BAW II, 4.

46 BAW I, 430.

All in all, Nietzsche was a disciplined and diligent pupil at Pforta. He acquired two new friends there: Paul Deussen, son of a Protestant pastor, and the Silesian Junker Carl von Gersdorff. His friendship with the latter was born from a common interest in music; we also owe Gersdorff the first testimony regarding Nietzsche's improvisations on the piano. 'Every evening, between 7:00 and 7:30, we met in the music room. His improvisations linger in my memory; I would like to believe that even Beethoven could not have improvised in a more gripping fashion than Nietzsche, especially when a storm was coming.'[47] Similar judgements were made by everyone who heard his fantasies at the piano. Deussen – who has entered the history of philosophy as a historian of Indian philosophy, as the translator of the Upanishads, and as the editor of Schopenhauer, to whom Nietzsche 'converted' him – relates in his *Memoir of Friedrich Nietzsche*:

> I no longer know what brought us closer together. I believe it was our common love for Anacreon, whose poems we were all the more enthusiastic about as third-year students, since their easy Greek put fewer difficulties in the way of understanding them. We recited his verses on walks together, and we made a friendship pact by coming together in a solemn hour . . . to replace the polite 'Sie', which was customary in Pforta even between the students, with the familiar 'Du' reserved only for closer friends; instead of drinking brotherhood, we took a pinch of snuff on it.[48]

---

47 Carl von Gersdorff, in Anon., 'Aus der Jugendzeit Nietzsches', *Weltchronik*, Bern, 21 January 1910.

48 Paul Deussen, *Erinnerungen an Friedrich Nietzsche* (Leipzig: Brockhaus, 1901), 3–4; Sander L. Gilman, ed., *Conversations with Nietzsche: A Life in the Words of His Contemporaries*, trans. David J. Parent (New York: Oxford University Press, 1987), 10 [translation modified].

Up to the end of Nietzsche's time at secondary school, Krug and especially Pinder remained his most important friends, whom he met up with during vacations and every time he returned to Naumburg.

Alongside detailed descriptions of the collective life of the students and stories about their common excursions and gay amusements, the private notebooks of the Pforta period show evidence of a profound adolescent melancholy, which Nietzsche would remember many years afterward: 'At Pforta, when the fields were deserted and autumn was coming'; 'Melancholy afternoon – religious service in the chapel at Pforta, faraway organ tones'.[49] 'The bitter feeling of autumn awakens in my soul', writes Nietzsche, not yet fifteen, in his Pforta journal. 'I still remember a day from last year, when I was in Naumburg. I was taking a walk down by the Marientor; the wind was blowing through the stubble fields, the yellow leaves were falling to earth, and the feeling shot through me so very painfully: the blossoming spring, the glowing summer – they are gone! Gone forever! Soon the white snow will bury dying Nature.'[50] And, a few days later:

> God, why have you given me such a heart, that I both enjoy and rejoice in Nature? I cannot bear it. Already the sun is no longer sending down its warm rays; the fields are empty and desolate, and hungry birds are already collecting food for winter. For winter! So close together are joy and sorrow, yet the passage between them is crushing . . . O Nature; you have wreathed my heart in bitter sorrow. Last rose! Weeping, I see you blossom and pass, with you I live and I perish, with you I will one day rise again! For the lovely dream of this life cannot

49 NF 11[11], 1875; NF 28[7], 1878.
50 BAW I, 121.

> sink down forever; someday I will drink again of spring's breath, spring's foam![51]

In the midst of these autumnal fantasies, which he is already attempting to stylize in a literary fashion, the young Nietzsche also sets himself the task of imagining 'how someone feels who does not have a homeland', and writes a poem entitled 'Without a Homeland'.[52] We encounter these 'states of soul' again in the grown man, in a poem dedicated to autumn, written in the summer of 1877 and revised in 1884 with the title 'In the German November', and in the 1884 poem 'Without a Homeland', neither of which he published.[53]

5. Toward the end of this period, in March 1862, we find the direction of the young Nietzsche's thought expressed with stupefying clarity in essays on 'Fate and History' and 'Free Will and Fate' which he wrote for his friends in the 'Germania' circle (Karl Löwith and Richard Blunck have already indicated the importance of these essays). We see traces in them of what he was reading during these years (Emerson and Feuerbach seem to figure most conspicuously), but the essential thing is the way Nietzsche attacks his theme, albeit hesitantly, and, so to speak, outlines the programme of his future philosophical quest as it will develop in its 'Nietzschean' particularity once he returns, after 1876, to what he himself always called his mission – that is, after his phase of preoccupation with Wagner, Schopenhauer and philology. To us this would seem the most significant aspect of these two youthful

51 BAW I, 129.

52 'Ohne Heimath!' BAW I, 122.

53 'Im deutschen November', NF 28[59], 1884; 'Ohne Heimath', KGW VII/4.2, 108 and 210.

essays. It is worth emphasizing that, here, Nietzsche also passed decisively from an artistic-intuitive perspective on life, which was not working for him as such (and which would never work for him), to historico-philosophical reflection.

Nietzsche does not conceal his uncertainty; he still hesitates to take an 'impartial and historically appropriate' position with regard to the religion of the fathers. 'An effort of this kind is not the work of a few weeks, but of a lifetime.' But 'it is the aim of all great ambitions to reach up to the heavens; the reign of Heaven on earth is practically the same thing'.[54] Yet, to him, these ambitions seem destined to fail: they draw the individual, whose fate is necessarily limited by 'childhood impressions, the influence of his parents, and his education', back to his childhood faith. Nonetheless, Nietzsche does not refrain from advancing with trepidation toward the perspective of the 'infinite', located at the limits of history and individual fate: 'Just as custom exists as the product of an era, a people, a spiritual tendency, so also is morality the result of a general development of humanity. It is the sum of all truths for our world.' Yet 'it is possible that in the infinite world it signifies nothing more than the result of a particular spiritual tendency in *our* world', and that from the particular truths of 'singular worlds' 'a universal truth' may develop.[55]

Nietzsche thus tries to resolve the problem of the relationship between free will and fate in a dialectical fashion: 'Fate is the infinite force of resistance against free will; free will without fate is inconceivable, just as spirit without reality, good without evil, are inconceivable . . . Perhaps free will is nothing more than the maximum potency of fate, just as the spirit is nothing other than infinitely minute substance, and good is the most subtle

54 BAW II, 55.

55 Ibid., 56.

development of evil itself.'[56] Indeed, we should not forget that fate is as much an abstraction as free will, 'which signifies the capacity to act consciously, while by the term fate we mean the principle unconsciously guiding our actions'. The two concepts are founded on the 'idea of individuality'; 'absolute freedom of the will, without fate, would make a god of man, the fatalistic principle would reduce him to an automaton'.[57]

In private notes of the same period, Nietzsche expresses his anti-metaphysical tendency even more clearly: 'That God became man indicates only that man should not seek his salvation in the Infinite, but that he should instead found his Heaven on earth. The illusion of a supramundane world had brought men to assume a false attitude toward the earthly world: this was the product of a childhood of the nations . . . Amidst grave doubts and struggles, humanity becomes virile: it recognizes in itself "the beginning, the middle, the end of religion".'[58] Twenty years later, Zarathustra would not have spoken differently.

A few months after the essays just mentioned, we find a trace of the 'Manfredian' abysses that Nietzsche recalled having sensed in himself at the age of thirteen in a fragment of a novella preserved in Stefan Zweig's famous collection of autograph manuscripts. It is perhaps not by chance that the novella bears the title *Euphorion*, since, in the second part of *Faust*, Goethe had represented the great Byron symbolically in the figure of Euphorion, and the text is important, if for no other reason than that documents of this sort are relatively scarce in the holdings of the former Nietzsche-Archive and simply do not appear in the unctuous biography by Elisabeth Förster-Nietzsche. Here is a nearly complete translation:

---

56 Ibid., 59.

57 Ibid., 62.

58 Ibid., 63.

The early morning red reverberates in the sky in a bright play of colours, a thoroughly burnt-out firework that bores me. My eyes sparkle quite differently, I fear they will burn holes in the sky. I feel I am completely released from my chrysalis, I know myself through and through and want only to find the head of my double to dissect his brain, or my own child's head with golden locks . . . oh . . . twenty years ago . . . child . . . child . . . the word sounds so strange to me. Was I too a child, turned in the lathe of the old worn-out world mechanism? And do I now – like a nag tied to a treadmill – complacently drag the rope we call fate until I rot, till the knacker buries me, and a few carrion flies ensure me some small measure of immortality? At this thought I feel almost like laughing – meanwhile, I am bothered by another idea: perhaps little flowers will grow from my bones, maybe a 'sweet violet' or even – provided the knacker relieves himself on my grave – a forget-me-not. Then lovers will come along . . . Disgusting! Disgusting! This is corruption! Still, I luxuriate in such thoughts of the future, for it seems more pleasant to me to rot in moist earth than to vegetate under blue skies, better to crawl as a fat worm than to be a human being – a wandering question mark. It always calms me to see people walk down the street, dressed in bright colours, groomed, dainty, merry people! What are they? Whitewashed graves is what they are, as some wag or another has said. In my room it is quiet as death . . . Before me an inkwell to drown my black heart in, a pair of scissors to get me used to slitting my throat, manuscripts for wiping myself, and a chamber pot. Across from me there lives a nun, who I visit occasionally to rejoice in her modesty. I know her very precisely, from her head to her toes, more precisely than I know myself. She used to be a nun, thin and delicate – I was a doctor and soon made her fat. Her brother lives in concubinage with her, he was too

> fat and rosy for me, I made him thin – like a corpse. He will soon die, which pleases me – then I will dissect him. First, however, I will write down the story of my life, for aside from the fact that it is interesting, it is also instructive for quickly making young people old . . . I am a master at that. Who should read it? My doubles, many of whom are wandering through this vale of tears. – At this point Euphorion leaned back a little and groaned, for he suffered from tuberculosis of the spine.[59]

Nietzsche sent this fragment to a school friend, Raimund Granier, on 18 July 1862, with these words: 'After I wrote the first chapter, taken by nausea I threw the plan for my disgusting novella into the sea. I am sending you this monstrous manuscript for you . . . to do whatever you like with it. Once I had written it, I burst out in a diabolical laugh. I don't expect that you will care to read the sequel.' Richard Blunck has seen in this a symptom of the restlessness and disorientation that struck Nietzsche during the 'crisis of puberty'.[60] We would call attention to the almost involuntary invocation of a lost childhood that opens Euphorion's perverse lucubrations. Aside from this, we note a certain straining for effect and a cerebral cynicism, which we do not encounter in any other writing by Nietzsche from these years (although, as Blunck observes, we cannot be certain that Elisabeth Förster-Nietzsche or even Nietzsche himself did not destroy further documents of this kind). It might seem a banal and superfluous observation, one hardly worth mentioning, to recognize the capacity of an eighteen-year-old youth to produce such perverse erotic images – though it is worth noting that their literary form is already an overcoming – were it not for the fact that Förster-Nietzsche and

59 Ibid., 70–1.

60 Blunck, *Friedrich Nietzsche*, 87.

her horde of devoted 'Nietzscheans' had undertaken the ridiculous and harmful (albeit successful) attempt to engender the legend of a 'little saint' who had never directly known the 'all-too-human' sides of life. Nietzsche himself certainly spoke in other terms. 'Two things are harmful', he would write fifteen years later: 'dull imaginary gratifications of a desire for vengeance, [and] living in erotic imagery that dirties fantasy and gradually gets out of hand, to the point where one's health is affected. Self-education helps here: both instincts must be satisfied in a natural way, so as to preserve the purity of the imagination. Renouncing vengeance and renouncing love make people sick, weak, and bad.'[61] But one searches in vain for this statement in Elisabeth Förster-Nietzsche's 'authorized' edition.

6. In his two final years at Pforta, Nietzsche worked hard, despite the turbulence and disquiet of adolescence. The crowning achievement of his high school years is an essay on Theognis, which he would rework and publish three years later at Leipzig.[62]

It is worth mentioning a commentary on the first chorus of *Oedipus Rex* written in the final year at Pforta, because, here, Nietzsche disconcertingly anticipates certain themes of *The Birth of Tragedy*.[63] At the end of this commentary, we find the following:

> From the observations made above, one recognizes a preeminent and peculiar quality of the tragedians: they were not only poets, they were also composers. What is more, they were both of these things, such that the one always accompanied the

61 NF 24[23], 1877; NF 23[29], 1876/77.

62 'Zur Geschichte der Theognideischen Spruchsammlung' (On the History of the Theognidean Collection of Maxims), KGW II/1, 1–58.

63 BAW II, 364–99.

> other; and if we take into account that according to ancient testimony they were masters of stage blocking, choreography, and the scenic art, as well as the fact that they were themselves actors, and indeed notable actors, then we might see in their works what the newest musical school [Nietzsche had already spoken in this essay of the 'genial reform plans of Richard Wagner'] has proclaimed as the ideal of the 'artwork of the future', works in which the most noble arts converge in harmonious fusion.[64]

Nietzsche left the Pforta school with a high school diploma at the beginning of September 1864. One of his best early poems stems from these days. It is dedicated to the 'unknown god' who digs into the depths of his soul, who shakes his life like a tempest.[65] By the end of Nietzsche's conscious life, the unknown god will also become an 'executioner-god' (*Dithyrambs of Dionysus*, 'Lament of Ariadne'). But, in these weeks of preparation for the new life of the university student, Nietzsche's mood was one of confidence and joyous expectation.

At the threshold of his university years, we also find evidence of an inward experience that Nietzsche would return to many years later: 'Near Bonn, where the Wied flows into the Rhine, I was overcome once again by the feeling of childhood'; 'At the age of seven – felt the loss of childhood. But at twenty . . . I felt like a child again.'[66] This moment of grace in recovering the feeling of childhood is easy to locate in time and space: precisely at twenty, on 16 October 1864, Nietzsche met his friend Paul Deussen at Neuwied (where the Wied flows into the Rhine) in order to travel

64 BAW II, 376–7.

65 BAW II, 428.

66 NF 11[11], 1875; NF 28[8], 1878.

together by steamer to Bonn, where they would spend their first year at university. We have a long letter dated 17 October from Nietzsche to his mother and sister, but it does not mention this inner experience; he seems not to have discussed it with Deussen or with anyone else. Not until eleven years later, while making a sort of list of important moments from his childhood and youth, does Nietzsche record, for himself, this recovered moment of a lost happiness.[67] The episode is so important that he returns to it again three years later, in the lines on his 'lost childhood' and the 'admonishing voice' of his father from the series of private notes cited above.[68]

The two semesters at Bonn – winter 1864/65, summer 1865 – were disappointing. Having joined a student corporation, the 'Franconia', Nietzsche soon found himself unable to bear the 'duties' of this association or the way of life of his schoolfellows: the loud and interminable drinking parties in the pubs, the uniform confusion of ideas which concealed the sure traits of future middle-class philistines behind an apparent nonconformity. Recalling this period some years later, he wrote:

> I left Bonn like a fugitive. When my friend Mushacke accompanied me to the bank of the Rhine to wait for the steamer to come from Cologne, I felt no melancholy within me on having to leave such a beautiful spot and such a pleasant countryside so as to rid myself of a host of young comrades. Indeed, it was the latter who had chased me away . . . My nature found no satisfaction in their company; I myself was still much too shy and withdrawn into myself, and I did not have the energy to play a role in the goings-on there. Everything was forced

67 NF 11[11], 1875.

68 *Memorabilia*, NF 28[1–60], 1878.

> upon me, and I did not succeed in mastering the environment I found myself in.[69]

Speaking again later, as a Basel professor, of the student corporations and of the communal life of the students in general, Nietzsche's judgement was milder: in all this he saw a sign of the fact that the academic youth did not receive any preparation for life from society or from its teachers. Thus, in Bonn, Nietzsche failed to draw much profit from university lectures; as we shall see, it was only the encounter with the rigorous critical and historical method of the philologist Friedrich Ritschl that would show him a way out of his inner confusion. He had enrolled as a student of theology and philology so as not to dash the hopes of his mother, who expected her son to become a Protestant pastor. But it was precisely at Bonn that Nietzsche, helped by David Friedrich Strauss's *Life of Jesus* and by the historical study of Christianity in general, decided to clarify his own position, regardless of anyone else, and to abandon the theological faculty.

The difficult disagreements with his mother in the spring of 1865 were surmounted through the decision never to speak of religious matters in her presence; for her part, Franziska Nietzsche had to resign herself to letting her son go his own way. In a letter to his sister of June 1865, Nietzsche calmly expounds his arguments, which culminate in these words: 'Is it tranquillity, peace, happiness we are after with our searching? No, we seek only the truth, even if it is supremely terrible and ugly . . . Here people part ways: if you want peace of mind and happiness, believe, if you want to be an apostle of truth, then seek.'[70]

---

69 BAW III, 291–2.

70 Letter to Elisabeth Nietzsche, 11 June 1865.

At Bonn in February 1865, an episode occurs that has kept Nietzsche's 'devotees' busy, as well as the great number of medical writers, psychiatrists and psychologists who have sought in his life some occasion to demonstrate or confute the syphilitic origin of his mental illness. Let us attempt to deal with this pseudo-problem once and for all. Paul Deussen, who spent those two semesters at Bonn with Nietzsche, wrote some thirty years later:

> One day in February 1865, Nietzsche had travelled to Cologne on his own, and there had engaged a guide to show him the sights of the city; he finally asked to be taken to a restaurant. The guide took him to a house of ill repute. 'Suddenly', Nietzsche told me the next day, 'I found myself surrounded by a half-dozen apparitions in tinsel and gauze looking at me expectantly. I stood speechless for a while. Then I instinctively went to a piano as if to the only soul-endowed being in the place and struck a few chords. That dispersed my shock and I escaped to the street.[71]

There is no reason to doubt Deussen's credibility or his good memory, as his student Richard Blunck has attested.[72] Nietzsche's behaviour is in fact neither surprising nor implausible, and the episode itself – let us repeat this for emphasis – would not be worth mentioning, had it not given rise to what Blunck has justly called a typical *querelle allemande*:[73] the debate on the question of whether Nietzsche, as a student in the 1860s, ever visited a bordello, and whether, during one of these visits, occurring *after* the one

71 Deussen, *Erinnerungen*, 24; Gilman, *Conversations with Nietzsche*, 24 [translation modified].

72 Blunck, *Friedrich Nietzsche*, 109.

73 Ibid., 110.

recounted by Deussen, he contracted a specific infection, which then, some twenty years afterward, became manifest, in its final stage, as progressive paralysis, and then as dementia. If we can accept this account of the facts as accurate, as well as the conclusions reached by Blunck, according to whom this was how the hypocritical climate of bourgeois morality long compelled young students to satisfy their 'erotic needs', then such a hypothesis seems plausible with regard to Nietzsche as well. The hypothesis is confirmed by a declaration that Nietzsche, already in a state of dementia, himself made at the sanatorium in January 1889, thus recorded: '1866 syphilitic infection'.[74] Based on the testimonies collected by the psychiatrist Lange-Eichbaum and on Nietzsche's own declarations, Blunck concludes that we must accept as certain the fact that Nietzsche's dementia 'can *only* have had its origin in a syphilitic infection', contracted however in Leipzig and culminating in a progressive paralysis.[75] Walther Vulpius, a doctor in Weimar who had occasion to treat Nietzsche's eyes between November 1899 and May 1900, came to substantially the same conclusion in an unpublished study of 1923.[76] The syphilitic infection is simply one element in the complex that we could call 'Nietzsche's illness', and of which there are other traces stretching back to childhood. A medical analysis of all the symptoms and all the crises of which there is evidence in Nietzsche's letters and writings or in the testimony of contemporaries, if it were possible, would be of purely biographical interest; but it is not necessary for

74 Jena clinical files, in Volz, *Nietzsche im Labyrinth seiner Krankheit*, 393.

75 Wilhelm Lange-Eichbaum, *Nietzsche. Krankheit und Wirkung* (Hamburg: Lettenbauer, 1947); Blunck, *Friedrich Nietzsche*, 161.

76 Walther Vulpius, in Sander L. Gilman and Ingeborg Reichenbach, ed., *Begegnungen mit Nietzsche* (Bonn: Bouvier, 1985), 256–8; also excerpted in Gilman, ed., *Conversations with Nietzsche*, 256–9.

understanding his thought, and it is even less useful for judging it. Both Nietzsche's devotees and his 'detractors' have, in the past, been united in attributing to syphilitic infection (or, as we saw earlier, to inherited illness) a significance that it could not have had either for Nietzsche's 'morality' or for his philosophy. This pseudo-problem is no longer of interest today.

7. On 17 October 1865, Nietzsche arrived in Leipzig in quite a different state of mind from the one in which, on a luminous autumn day in Bonn a year prior, he had 'felt like a child again' and had seen 'the Rhine with the free and proud feeling of an indescribably rich future'.[77] This time, he had behind him the bitter consciousness of a wasted year.

One of the motives that had led Nietzsche to change universities had been Friedrich Ritschl's decision to leave Bonn on account of a longstanding conflict with his colleague Otto Jahn, which had ended in a complicated and sensational academic feud. Many other students demonstratively left Bonn to follow Ritschl to Leipzig. A student of Gottfried Hermann and of Carl Reisig, a friend of Arnold Ruge in Halle between 1831 and 1833, in close contact with the romantic A. W. Schlegel during his years at Bonn and with the great scholar of Greek religion Friedrich Gottlieb Welcker, founder together with Theodor Mommsen of a monumental collection of Latin inscriptions, the *Corpus inscriptionum latinarum*, editor of Plautus, author of foundational studies of the Alexandrian libraries and of the Greek grammarians, teacher of a great number of illustrious philologists (among the ones Nietzsche knew or had to do with were Hermann Usener and Jacob Bernays, Otto Ribbeck and Curt Wachsmuth), Friedrich Ritschl (1806–76) was not only one of the greatest philologists but also one of

77 NF 11[11], 1875; letter to Carl von Gersdorff, 11 October 1866.

the most fascinating academic 'masters' that the nineteenth-century German university had to offer.

Ritschl's personal influence on Nietzsche's life is rivalled only by that of Richard Wagner.

Friedrich Ritschl adhered with his entire being 'to the historical tendency, to the historical mode of considering human things'.[78] Using Schelling's *Lectures on the Method of University Study* to define philology's scope at the beginning of his academic career, Ritschl affirmed that philology belongs to the historical sciences and to the 'science of the human spirit', in contradistinction to the 'science of nature': 'Its object is the life of the mind, the cultural life of classical antiquity. We can define philology as Greco-Roman cultural history.'[79] In the contest between the 'philologists of the word' (*Wortphilologen*) and the 'philologists of things' (*Sachphilologen*), ongoing during his youth, Ritschl had taken a stand against the rigoristic one-sidedness of his teacher Gottfried Hermann (who had considered 'language' philology's exclusive object) without however blinding himself to the methodological failings of the 'philologists of things' (August Böckh, Friedrich Gottlieb Welcker, Karl Otfried Müller). According to Ritschl's programme, philology had to 'embrace the singular manifestations of literature as a continuous chain of natural processes of intellectual development, necessarily conditioned by the sum total of political, religious, artistic, scientific and practical formations, and variously nuanced by the local and temporal influences of outward life'.[80]

---

78 Letter to Nietzsche of 14 February 1872 on receipt of *The Birth of Tragedy*.

79 Otto Ribbeck, *Friedrich Wilhelm Ritschl*, vol. I (Leipzig: Teubner, 1879), 330.

80 Friedrich Ritschl, *Opuscula Philologica*, vol. 5 (Leipzig: Teubner, 1879), 151–2.

Ritschl had an exceptional ability to transmit his scholarly enthusiasm to students, to spur them to the acquisition of a sense of history, to the asceticism of the philological method and to the exercise of the critical spirit. No scholarly labour was too humble in his eyes: to Nietzsche, for instance, he entrusted the compilation of an analytical index of about twenty years of the *Rheinisches Museum*, the famous philological journal he edited.

The influence of the teacher can be felt both in Nietzsche's personal notes and in his letters from Leipzig during this period. At Ritschl's suggestion, a group of students, Nietzsche included, had founded a 'philological association', which met periodically to hear and discuss the results of the philological labours of each participant. On 18 January 1866, Nietzsche delivered the first paper, on the final redaction of the fragments of Theognis, which was much appreciated by his young colleagues. Encouraged by this success, he gave it to Ritschl to read. A few days later – precisely on 24 February 1866, as we know from other sources – Nietzsche was summoned by Ritschl to his house:

> 'What did you intend to do with this work?' I responded simply that as a lecture to our association it had already fulfilled its purpose. Then he asked me how old I was, where I was in my studies, and so on, and when I had answered him, he said that he had never seen anything like this from a third-semester student in the way of methodological stringency or sureness of combination. Then he emphatically prompted me to rework the talk into a small book and promised me his help in procuring some collations. After this scene my pride knew no limits.[81]

81 BAW III, 300.

After this day, the relationship with Ritschl became closer. Nietzsche often visited Ritschl at home to talk with him at his desk piled high with books and papers, on which there was always a glass of red wine. Ritschl's conversation was very animated, turning not only on scholarly problems but also upon his preoccupations at the university, the manoeuvres of his enemies, the manias of professors. He expressed himself with great freedom on all these subjects before the young student. But Nietzsche also wrote: 'He certainly overestimated his discipline, and for that reason he did not like the idea of philologists having much to do with philosophers. He tried to make his students useful for scholarship as quickly as possible; thus he tended to stimulate, sometimes too much, the productivity of each one of them. Nonetheless he was free of any *credo* in science. What bothered him especially was uncritical and unconditional faith in one's own results.'[82]

Several weeks before 'being born as a philologist',[83] Nietzsche had become acquainted with the philosophy of Schopenhauer, whose principal work, *The World as Will and Representation*, he had acquired from an antiquarian bookseller. Nietzsche would later describe two other authors as decisive discoveries in his life: Stendhal in 1879, Dostoevsky in 1885. But there is no doubt that the encounter with Schopenhauer's philosophy in the winter of 1865–66 was the most consequential intellectual event of the three. It also occurred at a time when Nietzsche was particularly turned inward upon himself, in the moment of concentration that followed the disillusionment with Bonn of which we have spoken. Writing two years afterwards, Nietzsche described the impression that his initial encounter with Schopenhauer had made on him:

---

82 Ibid., 305.

83 Ibid., 300.

> Every line screamed renunciation, negation, resignation; here I saw a mirror in which I perceived the world, life, my own soul in a terrible majesty. Here the disinterested eye of art beheld me, here I saw illness and healing, banishment and refuge, hell and paradise. I was violently seized by the need for self-knowledge, as well as for self-corrosion; the troubled and melancholy pages in my journal of that time, full of useless self-reproaches and the desperate mirage of a sanctification and transformation of the whole core of my being, are evidence of this. Dragging all my qualities and ambitions before the tribunal of a gloomy self-contempt, I became bitter, unjust and unrestrained in the hatred I directed against myself. Nor did I spare myself physical punishment. I forced myself to go to bed at two in the morning and wake up at six, fourteen nights in a row. I was seized by a nervous excitement, and who knows what degree of insanity I might have arrived at if the seductions of life, of vanity, and of the compulsion to regular study had not worked to counter it.[84]

This still fairly immediate description of the effect of reading *The World as Will and Representation* is notably different from the more famous one that we find nine years later in the third *Unfashionable Observation*, where the memory plays a part in the argumentative structure of the whole essay, and in which the preoccupations of 'Nietzsche as educator' integrate the reading of Schopenhauer into a general plan of cultural reform under the sign of Wagner.

In any case, Nietzsche appears to find an equilibrium between Schopenhauer's philosophy and the painstaking practice of philology. Indeed, philology is fitted into the new attitude to life that

84 Ibid., 298.

Nietzsche feels emerging in him in this period, as if by natural consequence: 'A young man should first of all throw himself into that state of astonishment that has been defined as the "philosophical pathos par excellence". Once life has dissolved itself before him into a series of enigmas, he should – deliberately, but with rigorous resignation – limit himself to that which it is possible to know, and make a choice from this vast field, according to his ability.'[85] Nietzsche's choice is philology.

8. Between the winter of 1865–66 and the summer of 1867, over the span of four university semesters, Nietzsche, newly 'born to philology', laboured with great application and success.

The fragments of Theognis, the sources of the lexicon of Suidas and of Diogenes Laertius's *Lives of the Philosophers*, a study of the tradition of the titles of Aristotle's works, Simonides's *Lament of Danae*, Homer and Hesiod – these are the principal themes of Nietzsche's independent works, some of which were published nearly immediately, others becoming the subject of later publications. For Nietzsche, acquiring expertise in philology had also a moral value. 'Every substantial work . . . has an ethical influence. The effort required to concentrate material and to shape it harmoniously is a stone falling into our inner life: the small circle becomes many more', writes the enthusiastic young philologist on 4 April 1867 to his friend Paul Deussen, who, under Nietzsche's influence, had given up theology to study philology in Berlin. And, as he did also with Schopenhauer, Nietzsche made passionate propaganda for philology during this period.

In this same period, Nietzsche becomes aware of 'not having a style' in German.[86] His ambition is to write his philological

85 Ibid., 297.

86 Letter to Hermann Mushacke, 20 April 1867.

works in at least a 'passable' style, rigorously setting out his proofs while avoiding the erudite pedantry of extensive citations.[87] His masters are Lessing, Lichtenberg and Schopenhauer. Admitting the effort that writing well costs him, he consoles himself by remembering that these three authorities on style 'unanimously affirm that it is difficult to write well, that nobody naturally possesses a good style, and that one has to work hard, against resistance, to acquire one'.[88]

As for the university lectures, what interested Nietzsche was primarily the method of instruction. He tried to learn how to become a teacher, because he himself wanted to become a true 'practical instructor', capable of awakening in his students 'the thoughtfulness and reflection that would enable them to keep an eye on the "Why? What? and How?" of their discipline'.[89]

The Leipzig years are certainly one of the few periods in which Nietzsche enjoyed a certain equilibrium and lived life with enthusiasm; his letters and autobiographical notes allow us to see him in regular contact with his beloved teacher Ritschl, intensely engaged in his work, at the centre of a small community of friends. If we did not chance to have evidence of a grave 'psychic imbalance' and if we were not already aware of Nietzsche's 'second life', we might almost say that he was happy at Leipzig. What is more, from just prior to the time in Leipzig we have a declaration by Nietzsche on the subject of 'happiness' that is worth our attention, because in another form and in infinite variations it will become the nucleus of his philosophical *ethos*: 'if happiness were truly desirable for man, the idiot would be the most beautiful

87 Letter to Paul Deussen, 4 April 1867.

88 Letter to Carl von Gersdorff, 6 April 1867.

89 BAW III, 297.

exemplar of humanity'.[90] Of his two Pforta friends, Paul Deussen had not followed Nietzsche to Leipzig, despite the latter's insistent invitations; Deussen had already had to put up with his friend's pedagogical mania at Bonn, and now – despite his affection and respect for Nietzsche – he did not feel inclined to be corrected and lectured at continually. In Carl von Gersdorff, the noble Silesian, Nietzsche found a considerably more 'malleable' nature, who recognized his superiority without rebelling. He and Hermann Mushacke – a friend acquired at Bonn – were the first to be converted by Nietzsche's propagandistic enthusiasm to the philosophy of Schopenhauer. Nietzsche and his friends frequently attended concerts and the theatre. In the summer of 1866, during the Austro-Prussian War, Gersdorff took part in the Prussian military campaign in southern Germany, while Saxony, allied with Austria, was occupied by Prussian troops. The good citizens of Leipzig, not paying much mind to the war, attended the theatre in droves, where a celebrated actress, Hedwig Raabe, did not fail to rouse their enthusiasm each evening. Nietzsche, too, who discovered the 'enraged Prussian' and Bismarck-admirer within himself during these weeks,[91] was among Raabe's admirers, and he may even have fallen in love a bit 'at a distance', to judge from the evidence of an extremely 'philosophical' letter of June 1866 in which he dedicated some of his songs to the beautiful Hedwig.

In the summer semester of 1867, that is, between Easter and August, Nietzsche and Erwin Rohde (1845–98) became friends. Nietzsche writes shortly thereafter:

> Without realizing it, but guided by a sure instinct, we would spend most of the day together. We did not work much, at least

90 Letter to Raimund Granier, second half of September 1865.

91 Letter to Franziska and Elisabeth Nietzsche, beginning of July 1866.

> not in the philistine sense of the word, but still we felt that we profited from every day that we spent together. This is the first time that I have had a friendship develop against an ethical-philosophical background . . . Usually we were at loggerheads; indeed, there was an extraordinary number of things we did not agree upon. But as soon as the conversation reached a deeper level, the dissonance of opinion evaporated, and we resonated in a calm and full harmony . . . I think with pleasure of that time we enjoyed together as artists, momentarily detached from the tumult and unrest of the will to life, given over to pure contemplation.[92]

Rohde expresses himself in similar terms in a letter to a mutual friend: 'Throughout the whole summer we led an extravagant existence, as if within a moving magic circle, not closing ourselves off to others in an unfriendly way, but still almost always alone together. We spent half days, even entire days together in a happy state of idleness, and I at least drew great profit from this two-voiced loafing, much more than any philological drudgery could have given me. Schopenhauer might have brought us together, but it was above all a vein of mutual sympathy that made a deep understanding possible.'[93] This is the first friendship between equals in Nietzsche's life; it is documented in one of the most beautiful exchanges of letters we have.

In the last months of the summer semester, the two friends lived together in the same house. At the end of June Nietzsche had decided to leave Leipzig in order to do his year of military service. In the first days of August, after having taken leave of their other friends and of their old teacher Ritschl, the two of

92 BAW III, 312–13.

93 Letter to Heinrich Wilhelm Wisser, 29 November 1867.

them took a trip together, mostly on foot, to the Bohemian Forest. At the end of their peregrinations, they visited Meiningen to hear a concert of the 'music of the future', with works by Hans von Bülow and Franz Liszt. On 28 August, they participated in the Wartburg festival, near Eisenach, where they heard Liszt's *Legend of St. Elisabeth*. At Eisenach, the two friends parted ways, Rohde heading for Hamburg and Nietzsche for Naumburg.

9. Having failed to gain permission to do his military service in Berlin, Nietzsche had to resign himself to spending his training period in Naumburg, living in his mother's house. He was assigned to the horse artillery. A photograph of the period shows him with a spiked helmet on a table, an unsheathed sabre . . . and glasses.

However, his military 'career' was abruptly broken off, after scarcely five months, by a fall from a horse that gave him a bad chest wound. The resulting infection and the required treatment lasted from the beginning of March to early August of 1868. Nietzsche was declared temporarily unfit for service. Decommissioned the day before his twenty-fourth birthday, he felt relieved to be out of uniform. He returned to Leipzig the next day to begin preparing for his doctoral exam.

During this year-long pause, whether on account of the obligations of military service or because he was forced into convalescence, Nietzsche meditated a great deal on his life, and particularly on his recently chosen vocation of philology. In his own mind, as well as in his friend Rohde's, the initial enthusiasm had increasingly given way to an extremely critical position with regard to academic philology. His letters from the period are full of reflections like this: 'we owe every enlightening idea in literary studies to the few great geniuses who live in the mouths of the educated . . . every good and productive accomplishment in the field of philology has been nothing more than the practical application of such typical ideas, and . . . the creative element in philological research is thus born from those who have done little or nothing in the way of philological study, while the famous works of philology were written by people devoid of any spark of creativity'.[94] Nietzsche's revisions of his studies on Democritus, planned as contributions to an unrealized *Festschrift* in honour of Ritschl, move in the direction of this 'bitter truth' to be told to philologists.[95]

Nonetheless, Nietzsche remained firm in his intention to dedicate himself to an academic career as a philologist. He explains his reasons for this decision in a letter to Rohde of 3 or 4 May 1868 in which he encourages his friend to imitate him: 'Anxious self-examination is hardly appropriate here: we *must*, simply because we cannot do otherwise, because we have no more appropriate career choice ahead of us, because we have blocked the path to other, more useful positions, because given our constellation of energies and ideas we have no other way of being productive for the benefit of our fellow man, if not by this particular path.'

Yet not even in his letters to Rohde did Nietzsche mention his intense inward debate with Schopenhauer during this period. He never did say 'everything' to anyone – neither to Rohde, nor to Overbeck, nor to Wagner, nor to Rée, to mention only the friends with whom he stood on terms of equality; and this explains the 'surprises' that Nietzsche always occasioned when one or another hidden thought came to light. There is thus no interpreter of Nietzsche who is 'authorized' by virtue of the sole fact of having been in more or less intimate contact with him. This could be the deepest significance of Nietzsche's so-called solitude.

In 1866, having just read *The World as Will and Representation*, Nietzsche acquired the most radical critique ever written of

94 Letter to Erwin Rohde, 1–3 February 1868.

95 Ibid.

Schopenhauer, by Rudolf Haym (1864).[96] Desiring to extend his understanding of philosophy, in the summer of 1866 he became acquainted with an important book: Friedrich Albert Lange's *History of Materialism* (1866), which made a great impression on him, moving him to occupy himself with Kant (albeit solely through the volume devoted to Kant in Kuno Fischer's *History of Modern Philosophy*, 1860), and awakening his interest in Democritus, to whom he devoted numerous essays both philological and historico-philosophical.[97] These essays arose between autumn 1867 and spring 1868, running parallel to several essays developing a critique of Schopenhauer, with Democritus figuring as a sort of anti-Schopenhauerian cipher.

Drawing on the work of another neo-Kantian critic of Schopenhauer, Otto Liebmann, Nietzsche focused his doubts on the Kantian 'thing in itself' (*Ding an sich*) as will and on the problem of the transition from the 'unicity of willing' to the individuation that is the precondition for intellectual knowledge.[98] 'Schopenhauer's attempt to base his explanation of the world on an assumed factor . . . is a failure.'[99] Schopenhauer had replaced what for Kant was unknowable – the 'thing in itself' – with the will, helped in this only by his poetic intuition. The attributes that Schopenhauer predicated of this thing in itself, that is to say of the

96 Rudolph Haym, *Arthur Schopenhauer* (Berlin: G. Reimer, 1864).

97 Friedrich Albert Lange, *Geschichte des Materialismus und Kritik seiner Bedeutung in der Gegenwart* (Iserlohn: Baedeker, 1866). Kuno Fischer, *Geschichte der neuern Philosophie*, vols III and IV: *Immanuel Kant* (Mannheim: Wassermann, 1860). These latter volumes are known to have formed part of Nietzsche's personal library, and all such volumes will hereinafter be identified with the abbreviation [NL].

98 Otto Liebmann, *Kant und die Epigonen. Eine kritische Abhandlung* (Stuttgart: Schober, 1865) [NL].

99 BAW III, 352.

will, are 'too determinate for something that is absolutely unthinkable'.[100] In sum: 'Schopenhauer wanted to find the x in an equation; and the result of his calculation is that it equals x: that is, he did not find it.'[101] In any case, 'the errors of great men are worthy of veneration, because they are more productive than the truths of small men'.[102] A few months later, in the autumn of 1868, Nietzsche 'updates' Schopenhauer, speaking of him as the philosopher of 'a regenerated Germany' (note the term 'regenerate', a favourite of Wagner's), of a 'reawakened classicity, a Germanic Hellenism'.[103] The accent is shifted to Schopenhauer's 'classical originality' and to the significance of his philosophy for a new culture. The themes of Nietzsche's Wagnerian utopia could not have been foreshadowed more emphatically.

Nietzsche's thinking on Democritus, however, develops in an entirely different direction. Nietzsche believes that Democritus has been done a great wrong, one that should be corrected:

> It is rare that an important writer has had to submit to so many attacks, for so many various reasons, as Democritus; theologians and metaphysicians have taken out on him their deep-seated anger at materialism; the divine Plato considered his writings so dangerous that he thought of burning them in a private auto-da-fé, and was restrained only by the thought that it was already too late, that the poison had already spread too far . . . Christianity, on its ascent, finally succeeded in carrying out Plato's energetic plan; in any event, in an anti-cosmic age the writings of Democritus and Epicurus could not but seem

100 Ibid., 354.
101 Ibid., 360.
102 Ibid., 353.
103 BAW IV, 213.

> the incarnation of paganism. Finally, it fell to our time to deny the man's philosophical greatness and to recognize in him the nature of a sophist.[104]

What, according to Nietzsche, was Democritus's project? He was the first Greek with a 'scientific attitude, which consists in striving to explain a great mass of phenomena *in a unitary fashion*, without having recourse in moments of difficulty to a *deus ex machina*'.[105] Democritus experienced dedication to science as 'a new life principle'. A 'scientific' life was the goal of any *eudaemonia*; thus

> he rejected the life of the masses and of the earlier philosophers. He traced the sufferings of men to their unscientific way of life, and in particular to their fear of the gods . . . He places an unconditional trust in the deductive power of *ratio*; he thinks it unveils the world and human beings to him, and thus he rejects the veils and the limits that others place on the same *ratio* . . . This way of looking at things had thus acquired an ethical value for him; he believed in the happiness of man, provided his scientific method was realized in the world; which should remind us of Auguste Comte. This faith made him a poet, although his doctrine itself did not include poetic elements.[106]

Nietzsche's familiarity with Comte can be traced to Lange's book, from which he transcribes this description of Comte's character: 'The noble Auguste Comte, a thinker and philanthropist who finished his days alone, struggling with poverty and

---

104 BAW III, 347.
105 Ibid., 348.
106 Ibid., 348–9.

gloom.'[107] (The 'great, honest Frenchman' Comte – see *Daybreak*, aph. 542 – will become a particular focus of interest for Nietzsche during his so-called positivistic phase.) Democritus is 'the father of all enlightening and rationalistic tendencies'; his is also 'a beautiful Greek nature, apparently cold like a statue, but full of hidden warmth'.[108] (At these words, the reader of Nietzsche cannot help but remember the pathos of the 'glaciers', of the icy heat of the 'free spirit'.) The life of Democritus is a 'martyrdom for science'; he is the 'Humboldt of the ancient world', and the 'only philosopher still alive'.[109]

In his philological studies on Democritus, Nietzsche encounters the key figure of Thrasyllus, the court astrologer who enjoyed the complete trust of the otherwise suspicious and sinister emperor Tiberius, and who was the collator and editor of the writings of Democritus. But Thrasyllus had also collated, into tetralogies, the writings of Democritus's 'enemy' Plato. Nietzsche found this astonishing: it was like a believer in the Bible simultaneously harbouring dangerous sympathies for the works of the materialists Ludwig Büchner and Jacob Moleschott. Nietzsche resolved the problem with the hypothesis that Thrasyllus had felt drawn to Democritus's purported Pythagoreanism.[110] What is of interest here is not so much what Nietzsche attempts to prove philologically as his description of Thrasyllus's personality, for which tradition had not given him any evidence. Thrasyllus becomes 'a shadowy, Faustian personality'; like Faust, feeling 'disgusted with science', he dedicates himself to 'astrology and magic'.[111]

107 Ibid., 365.
108 Ibid., 347; 349.
109 Ibid., 347; 364.
110 Ibid., 368.
111 BAW IV, 61; BAW III, 366.

Thrasyllus is 'one of those mysterious natures that we frequently perceive in the twilight of a dying old world and a dawning new one'.[112] Described in such modern terms, this duplicity of Thrasyllus could symbolize the duplicity of Nietzsche himself.[113] Friedrich Albert Lange represented a theoretical orientation that differed completely from that of Schopenhauer – not materialistic, to be sure, but rigorously agnostic and anti-metaphysical. In any case, at the end of August 1866 Nietzsche wrote to Gersdorff summarizing and accepting Lange's findings; however, he concluded that even from the most rigorously critical point of view 'we can still keep our Schopenhauer, indeed he has nearly become something greater for us', something like the music of Beethoven or the paintings of Raphael, beyond all refutation, an 'edifying' philosopher. On 16 February 1868, writing to Gersdorff about his study of Democritus, Nietzsche returns once again to Lange's *History of Materialism*, describing it as 'a book that delivers infinitely more than the title promises and which one can return to and reread again and again, a true treasure . . . I have resolved absolutely to get to know this man, and I intend to send him a copy of my essay on Democritus as a sign of my gratitude.' The notes on Democritus cease almost entirely after the spring of 1868; from those of a philological character Nietzsche draws the material for a minor publication of analects on Diogenes Laertius, in 1870.[114]

10. After his military service, Nietzsche reestablished himself in Leipzig, no longer as a student but as a *Privatgelehrter*. In the meantime, another essay he wrote on the sources of Diogenes Laertius

112 BAW III, 366.

113 Carl Roos, *Nietzsche und das Labyrinth* (Copenhagen: Gyldendal, 1940).

114 KGW II/1, 169–90.

had won a prize awarded by the University of Leipzig.[115] He delivered several more reports on his work at the Leipzig Philological Society; Friedrich Zarncke's *Litterarisches Zentralblatt* published several of his book reviews.[116] He was a frequent guest at Ritschl's house and at that of the orientalist Hermann Brockhaus, who had married a sister of Wagner's. Nietzsche himself lived near Karl Biedermann, a historian, publicist and Liberal professor at whose house artists and literati gathered regularly. Here Nietzsche met, among others, Heinrich Laube, who had recently become the director of the Leipzig theatre.

Meanwhile, his critical attitude toward the music of Wagner had gradually yielded to a true state of rapture. A little less than a month after returning to Leipzig, Nietzsche would meet Wagner personally, at the home of Hermann Brockhaus. He tells of that great and – as we shall see – fateful evening in a letter of 9 November 1868 to Erwin Rohde:

> I was introduced to Richard and I said a few words of veneration; he asked in detail how I had come to know his music, said terrible things about all the performances of his operas, excepting only the celebrated ones in Munich, and made fun of the conductors who jovially call out to their orchestras: 'Here, gentlemen, passion!' 'My dear fellows, a bit more passionately!' W. very much enjoys imitating the Leipzig dialect . . . This evening offered . . . pleasures of such a uniquely exciting kind that still today I am still having trouble getting myself back on track . . . Before and after dinner Wagner played all the important parts of the *Meistersinger*, imitating all the voices, all very spontaneously. He is an extraordinarily vigorous and

115 KGW II/1, 75–167.

116 Ibid., 365–79.

> fiery man who speaks very rapidly; he is very witty, and can make a private gathering such as this into a very merry affair. I had a long discussion with him about Schopenhauer. You will understand what a pleasure it was for me to hear Wagner speak about him with an absolutely indescribable warmth: what he owed to him, why he was the only philosopher to have understood the essence of music. Then he asked what today's professors thought of him, laughing a great deal about the philosophers' congress in Prague . . . Afterwards he read out a piece of the autobiography he is writing, an extremely amusing scene from his student life in Leipzig, which makes me laugh now just to think of it; what is more, he writes with great wit and skill. – Finally, as we were both making ready to leave, he shook me warmly by the hand and invited me in the most friendly manner to visit him to make music and philosophy.

From this moment on, Nietzsche was a Wagnerian.

More a Wagnerian than a Schopenhauerian, because – as one can see from his philosophical essays – Nietzsche had already arrived at a more distanced attitude toward Schopenhauer's philosophy, whereas getting to know the man Wagner literally overwhelmed him. A few months later, beginning in the spring of 1869, when he was also living in close personal contact with Wagner, Nietzsche imagined himself as a propagandist for cultural renewal under the sign of Schopenhauer's philosophy and Wagner's art. This was a very important 'utopian' phase of Nietzsche's development. However, it was possible only as an 'overcoming' – one more desired than real – of a certain way of doing philosophy, a process already underway by 1867 and in which it was neither the 'artist's metaphysics' of Schopenhauer nor the ideals of Wagner that played the main role, but rather a 'passion of knowledge', without limits and without 'veneration', which we will recognize presently in the Nietzsche of *Human, All Too Human* and *Daybreak*. This is, moreover, the Nietzsche whose voice can be heard, in a cryptic form, in the background of all his works of aesthetic utopia, up to the moment of highest utopian and propagandistic pathos (*Richard Wagner in Bayreuth*, 1876), in which coexistence will be transformed, indeed has already been transformed, into insoluble conflict and unbearable contradiction, and Nietzsche returns – as he himself said – to his 'vocation', which will consist primarily in a 'liberation of the spirit'.[117] Nietzsche thus again takes up the thread of 'radical' meditation, which does not know – or does not want to know – any passion other than the 'passion of knowledge'.

Several weeks after that November evening in 1868 when Wagner had invited his young friend to come and visit him, an unexpected twist of fate brought Nietzsche to Basel, not far from Tribschen, where Wagner had been living with Cosima von Bülow since 1867.

In early December of 1868, the chair of Latin and Greek literature at the University of Basel had become vacant because its occupant, Adolf Kiessling, was called to Hamburg. Kiessling, a student of Ritschl's, turned to his former professor to ask about Nietzsche, whose articles in the *Rheinisches Museum* had caught his attention. Ritschl replied: 'I have seen a great many young talents develop under my eyes in my thirty-nine years of teaching, but I have never known – or tried, to the best of my ability, to advance in my discipline – *such* a precocious, mature young man as this Nietzsche . . . If, God willing, he should live a long life, I prophesy that someday he will stand at the very forefront of German philology.'[118] Kiessling

117 *Ecce Homo*, 'Human, All Too Human', 3.

118 Johannes Stroux, *Nietzsches Professur in Basel* (Jena: Frommann, 1925), 32–3.

passed this information on to Wilhelm Vischer-Bilfinger, councillor of education in the government of the city of Basel. The latter had already written on his own account to six of the most influential German professors asking for names of young philologists suitable to fill the empty chair, and Hermann Usener, in Bonn, had also named Nietzsche in his reply. At this point Vischer turned directly to Ritschl, who repeated his assessment of Nietzsche with yet greater warmth. On 16 January 1869, Nietzsche could communicate the news of his appointment to Rohde with near certainty. On 12 February, the 'Lesser Council' of the city of Basel made the unanimous final decision.

Nietzsche was overwhelmed by this unexpected event and enjoyed it. His mother and sister were so taken by an understandable enthusiasm that Nietzsche lost patience. His friends in Leipzig rejoiced endlessly. In fact, Nietzsche's appointment at Basel surpassed the highest ambitions that a young philologist, still lacking a doctorate, could nurture. Nonetheless, alongside expressions of an intention to meet the new situation with dignity, Nietzsche's letters and private notes reveal a sort of resignation to fate. But not even Nietzsche's sceptical reflections on the 'not at all extraordinary' fact that, simply, 'a new professor has been born in the world', nor his remarks on 'solitude' and on the effort awaiting him in Basel, could make his relatives and friends think that he was anything less than satisfied, or that he had been visited by sinister apparitions.[119] Yet it was, in fact, during this period – early in 1869 – that something occurs which has been interpreted as a 'hallucination'. Nietzsche writes in one of his notebooks: 'What I fear is not the ghastly figure behind my chair, but its voice; also not the words, but the horribly inarticulate and

119 Letter to Franziska and Elisabeth Nietzsche, second half of February 1869.

inhuman tone of this figure. If only it spoke as humans do!'[120] The notebook in which these lines appear is otherwise filled with normal philological notes, and it is not the case – as those who first published it (in 1940) seem to believe – that the handwriting reveals a particular state of excitement. The writing is identical to that of the other notes, and even the punctuation – which is elsewhere sometimes imperfect or summary – is here irreproachable. Was Nietzsche thus describing, with extreme equanimity, something that was happening to him? Even in this case, it is hardly useful to turn to psychopathology, and the term 'hallucination' adds nothing to the decidedly elusive meaning of these sinister and mysterious lines. It may however be useful to remember that several years later, and in a context whose significance is easier to grasp, Nietzsche spoke of the 'voice of history' and wrote (citing Faust's nocturnal monologue): 'Terrible vision! I cannot bear your sight!'[121]

On 23 March, Nietzsche was awarded a doctoral degree by the philological faculty at Leipzig based on the essays he had published in the *Rheinisches Museum*. On 17 April, he relinquished Prussian citizenship to become a Swiss citizen. At two in the afternoon on 19 April 1869, Nietzsche arrived in Basel.

---

120 BAW V, 205.

121 NF 5[194], spring 1875, and *Human, All Too Human*, I, aph. 233. [The quotation is from the scene in which Goethe's Faust summons the Earth Spirit (*Faust*, lines 482 and 485). Trans.]

2
The Basel Years (1869–79)

1. In Basel, Nietzsche was a diligent teacher, both at the university and at the Pädagogium (an equivalent of the Italian classical lyceum). The many memoirs left by his students describe him as a humane instructor, capable of moving even the laziest to study. Nietzsche frequently used the extemporaneous reading of classical texts, a practice followed at Pforta, to transmit real knowledge of antiquity, rather than commonplaces. We still have the manuscripts of his university lectures. It is difficult to tell from them to what extent he went beyond factual information. Naturally, we find hints here and there of things he would later say in his works. But the teaching notebooks will forever remain a mere written trace of something that was intended for oral expression. Nietzsche reflected a great deal on the problems of educating young people, on the function of 'cultural institutions', and he felt the necessity of educational reforms, but his pedagogical ideals formed part of a much vaster vision of cultural reform – that is, they participated in the illusions he nourished during his years in Basel.

This is what formed his life's centre of gravity. The Franco-Prussian War interrupted his teaching activities for several weeks: Nietzsche, too, was caught up in the general enthusiasm of his nation and wanted to participate in the war. He could do so only as a medic, because he had just become a Swiss citizen. After a few weeks, dysentery and diphtheria put an end to this martial intermezzo. The consequences of the German victory and unification would inspire doubts and diffidence in him shortly thereafter; the events of the Paris Commune profoundly shook him (as they did Burckhardt), above all on account of the false report of the burning of the Louvre by the Communards. However much his colleague Burckhardt may have detested Wagner and his music, Nietzsche still felt profound sympathy and veneration for the great Basel historian. These feelings about Burckhardt would remain a constant throughout his life; meanwhile, Burckhardt tended to a certain reserve in his interactions with Nietzsche. During these first Basel years, they were united in a love for Schopenhauer and a shared conception of Greek civilization deriving from similar sources, which produced a dynamic of mutual influence. They had in common a critical attitude toward Bismarck's Reich, which, for Nietzsche, would later become a veritable 'antigermanism'. More important, however, was what Nietzsche himself called the 'feeling of an autumn of civilization'.[1] It suffices to read Burckhardt's letters to his friend Friedrich von Preen, or those of Flaubert to George Sand, or the *Philosophical Dialogues* of Ernest Renan, the last two of which Nietzsche knew, and all of which give the feeling that the year 1870 and then especially the Paris Commune represented a major event for all European intellectuals.[2] With diverse results: the wise resignation of Burckhardt ('the Spirit that grows from the ruins'), Flaubert's nihilism, Renan's scientistic and reformist aristocratism are so many elements with which Nietzsche

1 NF 28[1], 1878.

2 Gustave Flaubert, *Lettres de Gustave Flaubert à George Sand. Précédées d'une étude par Guy de Maupassant* (Paris: G. Charpentier et Cie, 1884) [NL]; Joseph-Ernest Renan, *Dialogues et Fragments philosophiques* (Paris: Calmann-Lévy, 1876). German translation: *Philosophische Dialoge und Fragmente* (Leipzig: E. Koschny, 1877) [NL].

would come into contact in his reflections on the 'autumn of civilization'. An entire tradition was evaporating along with all of its institutions, and – we would add from today's perspective – a new tradition was forming, far beyond what these writers could anticipate or diagnose, Nietzsche included.

To understand how Nietzsche was thinking about the European crisis at this point, it is worth reading the letter he wrote to his friend Carl von Gersdorff on 21 June 1871:

> Beyond the conflict of nations, what we have found shocking is the sudden and terrible emergence of that international Hydra's head, appearing as a harbinger of quite different future conflicts. If we could discuss this in person sometime, we would agree that our modern life, indeed all of old Christian Europe and its State, but above all the Latin 'civilization' now dominant everywhere, reveal the enormous flaw that inheres in our world: how, with our common past, we are all *responsible* for the emergence of such horrors, so that it does not behove us to get on a high horse and impute the crime of a struggle against culture to these unfortunates alone. I know what it means, the struggle against culture. When I heard of the fires in Paris, I was completely shattered for several days, and beside myself with tears and doubts: the whole scholarly and philosophical-artistic life seemed absurd to me, if a single day could eradicate the most glorious works of art, indeed entire periods in art history; with earnest conviction I held on for dear life to the metaphysical value of art, which cannot exist simply for poor humans' sake, but which has a higher mission to fulfil. Yet even in my moments of greatest pain I could not throw a stone at these blasphemers, who were for me but the carriers of a general guilt that invites much reflection!

The perspective of 'culture' (*Kultur*) is decisive for Nietzsche, and, by 'culture', he means what Burckhardt, too, had been expounding in his lectures on the study of history, which Nietzsche attended in the autumn of 1870: a power essentially antagonistic to the state, and in general to all established public powers. According to Burckhardt, culture 'continually acts to modify and subvert the two stable life institutions [that is: the state and religion], except in so far as these limit it by completely subordinating it to their purposes; if not, culture is critique of both [state and religion], the clock that strikes to let us know that in both, form and content no longer coincide'.[3] Nietzsche's letter contrasts 'culture' with Latin 'civilisation', following an antithesis that, as a philologist, he will have found in the writings of the great classical scholar Friedrich August Wolf (1759–1824). Yet Nietzsche modifies the content of the two concepts, for Wolf had contrasted the 'bourgeois policing, or civilization' attained by the peoples of the ancient East (Egyptians, Hebrews, Persians) with the 'higher intellectual culture proper' of the Greeks, *but also of the Romans*.[4] Now Latin (that is to say, French) 'civilisation' could only mean the modern bourgeois civilization responsible for the evils of the present day, and thus also for the proletarian insurrection in Paris, whose protagonists were, for Nietzsche, 'the carriers of a general guilt that invites much reflection'. This is as far as the university professor Nietzsche is able to comprehend a phenomenon completely exceeding his notions of social history: and let us not forget the 'international Hydra', the

3 Jacob Burckhardt, *Über das Studium der Geschichte*, ed. Peter Ganz (Munich: Beck, 1982), 276.

4 Friedrich August Wolf, *Darstellung der Alterthumswissenschaft, nebst einer Auswahl seiner kleinen Schriften und literarischen Zugaben zu dessen Vorlesungen über die Alterthumswissenschaft*, ed. S. F. W. Hoffmann (Leipzig: Lehnhold, 1833), 12.

International of Marx and Engels, which up to this point had held most of its congresses in Switzerland (in 1866 at Geneva, in 1867 at Lausanne and – in September 1869 – in Basel, where Nietzsche had then been living for several months). On the other hand, not many German university professors approved of the Paris Commune: the only exception is the *Privatdozent* Eugen Dühring in Berlin, a well-known muddlehead, with his combination of socialism, anti-semitism and anti-Marxism! Nietzsche sought salvation from modern bourgeois civilization in the 'metaphysical value' of art, but also – like his friend and comrade in arms Richard Wagner – in the 'German mission' (for the moment distancing himself, in this regard, from Burckhardt). Thus we read in the same letter to Gersdorff: 'if there is one thing we may retain in peacetime from this wild war game, it is the heroic yet circumspect spirit that I have found, to my surprise, so to speak as an unexpected discovery, fresh and forceful, with ancient German vigour, in our army. We can depend on that: we are permitted to hope again! Our *German* mission is not yet finished! I feel more courage than I did before: for all is not yet subject to French-Jewish [!] superficiality and "elegance" and to the greedy hustle and bustle of the "now-time" [*Jetztzeit*].' Wagner could not have put it differently, while, some fifty years later, in his *Reflections of a Nonpolitical Man* (1918), Thomas Mann would hark back to this set of antitheses – 'French' and 'German', *civilisation* and *Kultur* – with different emphases, but still under the sway of Schopenhauer, Wagner and Nietzsche.

But was Nietzsche then completely 'Wagnerianized'?[5] Yes, at least between 17 May 1869, the date he first visited Tribschen, and the other May day, in 1872 – the 22nd, Wagner's birthday – when he attended the groundbreaking ceremony of the theatre at Bayreuth and then the performance of Beethoven's Ninth

5 NF 41[2], 1885.

Symphony, conducted by Wagner. Left alone after the 'Tribschen idyll' had ended, he began to have ever-increasing doubts about the 'German mission' and the capacity of Wagnerian art to bring about reform, doubts partly arising earlier, but always overcome by the irresistible fascination of direct contact with Wagner's personality. A peerless actor and man of the theatre, a revolutionary and adherent of Feuerbach in the first half of his life and in the second a reformer through art and a Schopenhauerian, an enemy of clerical obscurantism but filled with sympathy for the Lutheran spirit, an enthusiastic admirer of Greek tragedy (the *Oresteia* of Aeschylus) and of Shakespeare, scornful of French 'elegance' and 'fashion' but a steadfast proponent of the 'German virtue' of the 'German youth' (Schiller), sincere and extroverted to the point of brutality in his personal relationships, capable of a contagious cheerfulness and hilarity but equally prone to stormy and irrepressible fits of anger, a lover of luxury and filled with compassion for the exploited working classes, generous to a fault with money (especially if he had received it as a gift), prepared to sacrifice anything and anyone to realize the 'idea of Bayreuth', a friend to animals and an enemy of the Jews – this was Wagner, the greatest 'artist' of his time, the last romantic genius to believe in his own genius. By his side in Tribschen, on Lake Lucerne, was Cosima, the illegitimate daughter of the Comtesse D'Agoult and Franz Lizst, who had left Hans von Bülow to follow Wagner; one of the most refined products of French Catholic education, transplanted into German culture, indeed into German Protestant culture (she never managed to write German without errors); endowed with superior intelligence and accustomed to interacting with the most influential personalities of her era in the arts and in literature, in music and the theatre; filled with faith in her mission 'in the service of a genius', but also an inflexible defender of his interests, ready to combat with intransigence any 'deviation' with regard to any of Wagner's ideas; a

Christian and a Schopenhauerian, religious to the point of superstition and a believer in miracles; cultivated, fascinating, disquieting, capable of great delicacy in friendships. Her letters to Nietzsche, perhaps even more than Wagner's (whose spokeswoman, however, she nearly always was) help us to comprehend why Nietzsche could write to Rohde in a letter of 3 September 1869: 'I too have my Italy . . . it is called Tribschen . . . dearest friend, I cannot express what I am learning and seeing, hearing and understanding there. Schopenhauer and Goethe, Aeschylus and Pindar are still living, believe me.'

2. The essential formulation of the problem that preoccupied Nietzsche during these Basel years can be found in the lecture he gave on 1 February 1870 on the subject of 'Socrates and Tragedy', one of the many writings preceding the publication of *The Birth of Tragedy*. Describing the figure of Socrates as a 'herald of science', Nietzsche says: 'science and the arts are however mutually exclusive'.[6] The identification of Socratism with nineteenth-century science is just as 'anti-historical' and arbitrary as Nietzsche's faith in the 'renaissance' of classical tragedy through Wagner's oeuvre. But this affirmation implies the future course of development that Nietzsche's thought would take and already anticipates his so-called positivistic period. In fact, the postulate that science and art mutually exclude each other holds both for Nietzsche as a Wagnerian and for Nietzsche the 'free spirit', only with opposite consequences.

The devaluation of 'Socratic' rationalism, as opposed to both Apollonian 'vision' and Dionysiac ecstasy, reaches its climax in *The Birth of Tragedy*. While composing the book, Nietzsche wrote to his friend Rohde at the end of March 1871: 'I am living

6 KGW III/2, 37.

in a more wanton state of estrangement from philology than could possibly be imagined . . . I am gradually transforming into a philosopher, and already believing in myself; indeed, if I were to turn into a poet, I would be prepared for that.' The thought that he could have said what he had written in the book on tragedy better as poetry can be found not only in the later self-critique with which he prefaced the book's reissue in 1886, but also in a private note by his friend Rohde from the time when Nietzsche was writing *The Birth of Tragedy*. According to Rohde, what spoke from the 'purple darkness' of Nietzsche's reflections on the origins of Greek drama was a 'metaphysics of art'. In the final pages of *The Birth of Tragedy* (chapter 24) we read: 'How can what is ugly and disharmonious, the content of the tragic myth, stimulate aesthetic pleasure? Here it becomes necessary to take a bold running start and leap into a metaphysics of art, by repeating the sentence written above, that existence and the world seem justified only as an aesthetic phenomenon. In this sense, it is precisely the tragic myth that has to convince us that even the ugly and disharmonic are part of an artistic game that the will, in the eternal amplitude of its pleasure, plays with itself.'[7] According to Nietzsche, this is the 'originary phenomenon' of Dionysiac art.[8] In the passage just cited we see traces of Schopenhauer, but also a decisive innovation that Nietzsche considered his 'freehold property', not yet transformed into 'mobile, current, minted property'.[9] This innovation consists in the fact that in Nietzsche the Schopenhauerian will is not negated in aesthetic contemplation, but rather justifies its existence as an

7 KGW III/1, 148; *Basic Writings of Nietzsche*, trans. and ed. Walter Kaufmann (New York: The Modern Library, 2000), 141 [translation modified].

8 [*Urphänomen*, a Goethean term. Trans.]

9 Letter to E. Rohde, 4 August 1871.

aesthetic phenomenon by 'playing with itself'. We know the great impression that reading Schopenhauer had made on Nietzsche in his student days, an impression owing above all to the 'ugliness' and 'disharmony' that Schopenhauer's description revealed in the 'world as will'. Nietzsche remained attached to this insight, even when not long thereafter, in 1868 – inspired by reading Friedrich Albert Lange, Otto Liebmann, and Kuno Fisher on Kant – he felt compelled to subject the theoretical basis of Schopenhauer's philosophy to critique. Already in *The Birth of Tragedy* Nietzsche's tendency is diametrically opposed to that of Schopenhauer, because instead of negating life, Nietzsche wants to justify it *entirely*, as it is, as an 'aesthetic phenomenon'. This is why his friend Rohde saw the book as a 'grand cosmodicy'.[10] Indeed, one could define Nietzsche's entire philosophy as a continual attempt at a cosmodicy. Here, too, then, as with the antagonism between science and art, we find a fundamental motif of Nietzsche's thought. We shall see that Zarathustra has his cosmodicy as well. We thus believe we are justified in asserting that Nietzsche's driving philosophical impulse can be sought in his will 'to say yes' to life, at any price and under any circumstances, even if evil and suffering never cease to arouse in him – even in pathological forms – the Schopenhauerian feeling of compassion.

The transformation of this 'freehold property' into liquid currency – that is, the application of this intuition of the Dionysian archetypal phenomenon to real life – would prove impossible. Over against the 'optimism' of the *Jetztzeit* ('now-time', an expression used by Schopenhauer to designate the 'modern era') – that is, against the values of the bourgeois society of his age – Nietzsche would exalt the society and the state of the Greeks.

The rebirth of the Germanic myth through Wagnerian drama

10 Letter from E. Rohde, 6 February 1872.

is the hope that Nietzsche expresses at the end of his book. But this hope was dissolving from within. Nietzsche knew that he had arrived at his vision of the Greek drama by means of philology, and that he was indebted to a particular philological and historical tradition: that of Friedrich and August Wilhelm Schlegel, Karl Otfried Müller, Friedrich Creuzer, Friedrich Gottlieb Welcker, Burckhardt, and also his teacher Friedrich Ritschl. Even if he was suffering from the 'historical malady', in the last analysis Nietzsche could not do without the 'historical sense'. This is the hidden meaning of the *Untimely Meditation* on history (1874), which despite all its pathos contains no indications as to how to 'cure' this illness. But that meant that modern man *could not* knowingly regain the 'closed horizon' of myth. Already in 1874, Nietzsche is seized by doubts regarding his Wagnerian hopes, not to speak of the hopes he had placed in Germanism, which had begun to evaporate beginning in 1873. To explain the phenomenon of Wagnerian art, Nietzsche returns – in 1874 – to the concept of the 'actor'. The actor has to 'lie' to create an illusion, but the 'affirmation of the illusion at all costs' (knowing that it is illusion, but passing it off as truth) is what Nietzsche would call, in the autumn of 1883 – referring explicitly to his Wagnerian period – his 'Jesuitism'.[11] It was not for nothing that Cosima predicted that her young friend would return to his philological studies, because 'with Schopenhauer, philosophy reached its limit'.[12] Yet Nietzsche continued to philosophize. Between 1873 and 1875, a subterranean development is completed in him that will lead him to write, in a private note of the summer of 1875: 'I have yet to express opinions that will be seen as *ignominious* for him who harbours them; even friends and acquaintances will become timid and

11 NF 16[23], 1883.

12 Letter to E. Rohde, 26 January 1873.

fearful. I will have to pass through this fire as well. Then I shall belong to myself all the more.'[13]

3. We do not know if Nietzsche read the *Night Watches* of Bonaventura, an early Romantic text of uncertain authorship, published anonymously in 1804. In the first of sixteen night watches, Bonaventura tells of the death of a free spirit, who – although a meddling priest attempts to convert him – dies 'like Voltaire'. Nietzsche dedicated *Human, All Too Human*, his book for 'free spirits', to Voltaire. To be sure, Nietzsche's work is very far from the naive and nearly idyllic stylization with which this romantic booklet describes the free spirit, who is closer – not only chronologically – to Voltaire and to Enlightenment philosophy than his Nietzschean epigone. The latter is born from 'the *peace of the disintegration*' of all the 'spiritual powers of the old, constrained world', and is, like Zarathustra later, a real, distinct character that Nietzsche makes speak, and who is thus not identical to Nietzsche *as a whole*, just as Zarathustra will not be the same as Nietzsche as a whole.[14]

The origins of the book for free spirits can thus be sought in a radical critical attitude characteristic of Nietzsche, one that never left him but which would turn into catastrophe when he later felt he had come to a dead end. 'There was a time when I felt nauseated with myself: the summer of 1876', Nietzsche wrote, while still in the midst of composing the first part of *Thus Spoke Zarathustra*.[15] Thus an interior emptiness, a disintegration of all 'ideals', the nullification of all metaphysical-artistic illusions are the precondition for Nietzsche's birth as a free spirit and hence for

13 NF 5[190], 1875.

14 NF 25[2], 1877.

15 NF 4[111], 1882–83.

his break with Wagner. He felt in conflict with his own 'scholarly conscience'. The fourth *Untimely Meditation*, *Richard Wagner in Bayreuth*, showed him preaching the gospel of Wagner at the height of what he called 'exaggeration', while the utopian mania for 'judging' everything and everyone in evidence in the *Untimely Meditations* now made him feel frankly 'ridiculous'.[16] Nietzsche clearly described the rupture provoked by his new book: 'I want to declare explicitly to readers of my earlier writings that I have renounced the metaphysical-artistic views that essentially informed their writing: these are pleasant, but untenable.'[17] The free spirit is thus also a 'noble traitor', because he abandons every 'conviction', every faith.[18] He also 'rises' above nations, customs and religions, above all the metaphysical illusions and artistic creations which – as 'the most salutary and beneficial of errors' – have shaped modern humankind.[19] History and psychological observation are his way of returning to these anterior phases of culture. He has the advantage of finding himself poised at the threshold between the past, with its religion, art and metaphysics, and the future, with its relationship to scientific knowledge. From this new perspective, Nietzsche perceives the illusions of the past as stages on the path to 'wisdom', the ideal of the free spirit: 'Our era is fortunate in that one can still, for a time, grow up within a religion, and have true access to art through music; this will be less easy for future epochs.'[20]

In any event, Nietzsche was aware of the difference between

16 NF 4[111], 1882–83.

17 NF 23[159], 1876/77.

18 NF 17[66] 1876.

19 NF 25[8], summer–autumn 1877; *First Untimely Meditation: David Strauss the Confessor and the Writer*, 1.

20 NF 23[160], 1876/77.

his 'freedom of the spirit' and that of the *esprits forts* of the eighteenth century. 'The image of the free spirit remained incomplete in the last century: they [the free spirits] negated too little and spared themselves too much.'[21] In this posthumous fragment he seems to understand freedom of the spirit, in the style of Voltaire, as inadequate, and to suggest the possibility of going beyond it. Another fragment from the same period speaks of the antagonism between the *esprits forts* and the 'man of the Church', the ecclesiastic or priest, both of whom however inhabit the same sphere, that of the *vita contemplativa*, now fallen into disrepute (that is, in the modern age).[22] This fragment ends with a somewhat enigmatic statement: 'a sort of renaissance of both [the cleric and the *esprit fort*] can now occur in a single person'. Was Nietzsche thinking of himself? In what sense does the Nietzschean 'free spirit' require the integration of the religious man, of a keeper of the faith? This is an isolated fragment, and thus difficult to understand precisely. In the final draft of *Human, All Too Human*, dictated later to Peter Gast, there is no sign that such a singular fusion might be possible. However, it is hard not to think of the 'pious atheist' Zarathustra.[23] In any case, both in his notes and in *Human, All Too Human*, Nietzsche repeatedly speaks of the need to revalue the *vita contemplativa*, that is, the life dedicated to gathering wisdom (Epicurus provides the classical model of this ideal), which involves both conscious limitation to the world circumscribed by experience (science, history, psychological observation) and a renunciation of action. The free spirit, moreover, is not 'productive': that is, he cannot be a poet or an artist; conversely, such 'productive' people will not be free spirits, for

---

21 NF 16[47]/16[55], 1876.

22 NF 16[51], autumn 1876.

23 *Thus Spoke Zarathustra*, IV, 'Retired'.

only religion or metaphysics, and not science, can give birth to poetry and art.[24] As far as action is concerned, Nietzsche delineates a sort of utopian portrait of the thinker of the future, in whom 'European–American' activism would be united with the 'Asiatic' contemplativeness of the Russian peasant. This combination would guide humanity toward the solution of the 'world enigma'. The task of the free spirits until that point is to break down all the barriers blocking a 'coalescence of humankind': 'religions, states, monarchic instincts, illusions of wealth and poverty, prejudices regarding health and race, etc.'[25]

4. In a deeper sense, however, the separation from Wagner signifies a condemnation of art, and not only of modern art. Nietzsche retains his 'aesthetic instincts', but on the one hand he historicizes them in order to comprehend the past, in which art joins religion as one of the two great powers, while on the other hand he criticizes the highest manifestation of art in his time, the art of Wagner, as the apex of the histrionic theatricality and the antipathy to science characteristic of 'poets'. Nietzsche becomes a critic of poetic productivity: as we have seen, the free spirit is not inclined to yield to the seductions of the creative instinct, of 'impure thought'.[26] In *Human, All Too Human I* (aph. 150) he says that the poets remain religious, even if poetry has its origins in the weakening of religion. The final words of the *Untimely Meditation* dedicated to Wagner (1876) signify as much: for the men of the future – who will have renounced art! – Wagner will be the 'transfigurer' of a past. The frankly subordinate function that Nietzsche assigns to art in *Richard Wagner in Bayreuth* prefigures motifs

24 NF 16[54], 1876.
25 NF 17[55], 1876.
26 NF 17[1], 1876.

from *Human, All Too Human*. One should take care, Nietzsche says, not to attribute to art a significance beyond affording a restorative pause in man's struggle against *necessity* (chapters 4 and 7). And let us not forget another moment that shows the insidious ambiguity of Nietzsche's taking leave of Wagner in this *Untimely Meditation*. Nietzsche underscores the reformist intentions of the Bayreuth enterprise (it is not for nothing that he alludes in this text to the notion of Wagner as a revolutionary influenced by Feuerbach), but it is precisely through this 'social' radicalization of Wagnerism that he prepares his retreat, so to speak, his desertion from Wagner's camp: because, in fact, Wagner had betrayed these intentions and had stooped to a compromise with the Reich and the Church, transforming the Bayreuth Festival into a bonfire of the vanities and of the ultramodern nervousness of a bourgeois and decadent Europe. Nietzsche thus seems to have purposely exaggerated his 'idealism' with regard to Wagner so as to put Wagner himself to the test, by a standard that Nietzsche knew to be higher than (or better yet extraneous to) the mentality of the 'perfect artist' Wagner. When he published the fourth *Untimely Meditation*, the theory of the 'impure thought' of poets and of artists in general was already worked out in his notebooks. Whereas in the era of *The Birth of Tragedy* the world required an aesthetic justification, now it was precisely the aesthetic powers of humanity that most distanced it from the truth. This is not to say that the world has some other 'justification': at this point, Nietzsche seems to think that the world is 'without meaning'. Now that religion and art have collapsed and 'metaphysical need' (which is, for Nietzsche, no longer 'eternal', but historically conditioned) has been frustrated, there is nothing left but the quest for an ideal of contemplative wisdom, precisely the ideal that Nietzsche sketched in the figure of the free spirit.

'Man is wise as long as he is seeking the truth; he is a fool if he thinks he has found it.'[27] Nietzsche adopts this maxim from a little-known seventeenth-century German writer, Paul Winckler (1630–86). A similar attitude, reminiscent also of Gotthold Ephraim Lessing, is expressed literarily in Nietzsche's choice of the form of the aphorism, which he perfected through diligent study, and which constitutes one of his strongest claims to a place in the history of German literature.

We know that Nietzsche was a tireless worker. His readers, especially those of his aphoristic works, run a risk of reading him badly and hastily on account of the 'facility' of his style and the inimitable clarity of these short compositions in prose, rarely longer than a single page, more often closer to half a page or only a few lines long. Whoever has cast a glance at his working notebooks knows that these texts are the fruit of a long, careful process of elaboration and chiselling. This necessitates a new way of reading Nietzsche's aphoristic works, a way of reading that, to be truly productive, cannot rest content with spontaneous enjoyment of the genial paradox or with 'aesthetic' pleasure, but which must, rather, plunge into the depths and attempt to perceive the heart of the creative process, as well as the effort that even the shortest of maxims required of their author. This must be a philological reading, of the kind Nietzsche himself invited when he wrote in his 1886 preface to *Daybreak*:

> A book like this, a problem like this, is in no hurry; we both, I just as much as my book, are friends of *lento*. It is not for nothing that I have been a philologist, perhaps I am a philologist still, that is to say, a teacher of slow reading: – in the end I also write slowly. Nowadays it is not only my habit, it is also to my taste – a malicious taste, perhaps? – no longer to write anything

27 NF 23[158], 1876/77.

> which does not reduce to despair every sort of man who is 'in a hurry'. For philology is that venerable art which demands of its votaries one thing above all: to go aside, to take time, to become still, to become slow – it is a goldsmith's art and connoisseurship of the word which has nothing but delicate, cautious work to do and achieves nothing if it does not achieve it *lento*. But for precisely this reason it is more necessary than ever today, by precisely this means does it entice and enchant us the most, in the midst of an age of 'work', that is to say, of hurry, of indecent and perspiring haste, which wants to 'get everything done' at once, including every old or new book: – this art does not so easily get anything done, it teaches to read well, that is to say, to read slowly, deeply, looking cautiously fore and aft, with reservations, with doors left open, with delicate eyes and fingers . . . My patient friends, this book desires for itself only perfect readers and philologists: *learn* to read me well![28]

There is no worse way to access Nietzsche's world – which is the world of his experiences, of the events and the currents of thought of his time, of his historical and critical reflections, of the things he read (and what a reader Nietzsche was!) – than to content oneself with 'immediate' reading. As his past reception has proven, this can only lead to misunderstandings and dogmatic interpretations.

5. When Nietzsche's friends became acquainted with the 'book for free spirits' in May 1878, their reaction was one of shocked surprise and consternation. The 'philosophy of scandal' was

---

28 *Daybreak*, Preface, 5; *Daybreak: Thoughts on the Prejudices of Morality*, ed. Maudemarie Clarke and Brian Leiter, trans. R. J. Hollingdale (Cambridge: Cambridge University Press, 1997), 5.

beginning to show its true face.[29] Nietzsche had become an 'apostate'. The true and proper break with Wagner began after this work was published. The initial response from Bayreuth was an icy silence and total rejection, as Nietzsche discovered through Wagner's adepts as well as the publisher Schmeitzner, who published not only all of Nietzsche's works but also the *Bayreuther Blätter*. Then, in the summer of 1878, Wagner used his journal to attack Nietzsche without mentioning him by name, claiming the rights of the 'genius' and of the 'poetic inspiration' despised by the free spirits against a 'historical criticism immersed in Judaism'.[30] In the winter of 1878–79, Cosima had a short exchange of letters with Nietzsche's sister in which she gave her resentment free rein: 'Your brother's book distressed me, I know he was sick when he wrote all these intellectually so very insignificant, morally so very deplorable sentences . . . I do not know the author of this work; your brother, however, who has given us so much to marvel at, him I know and love, and that continues to live within me. With all his views (for example also about the Jews), he has joined a very well organized faction . . . May this treachery bear its author fine fruit!'[31] The incomprehension was thus total; what is more, Cosima thought she saw mean-spirited personal references in some of the aphorisms. She also appears to have been the most tenacious in her hostility to Nietzsche, if it is in fact the case, as Curt von Westernhagen affirms, that she was the one to block an attempt to reconcile Wagner and Nietzsche.[32]

29 Hugo Fischer, *Nietzsche Apostata, oder Die Philosophie des Ärgernisses* (Erfurt: Verlag Kurt Stenger, 1931).

30 Richard Wagner, 'Publikum und Popularität', *Gesammelte Schriften und Dichtungen*, vol. X (Leipzig: Fritzsch, 1888), 61–90.

31 KGW IV/4, 62 and 65.

32 Curt von Westernhagen, *Richard Wagner. Sein Werk, sein Wesen, seine Welt* (Zurich: Atlantis Verlag, 1956).

In reality, the break was irreparable. Above all, on the level of ideas: this was the price that Nietzsche had to pay once he had decided to abandon the 'metaphysical-artistic illusions' that tied him to Wagner. Wagner, for his part, could not show understanding for a way of thinking that aimed to demolish the rationale for his whole existence as an artist and which had come from the very person to whom he had been able to say, at one point, that he came second only after his wife, and that he was 'the only one . . . who knows what I want!'[33] No one can doubt Nietzsche's right to 'become what he was', following the promise he makes in the third *Untimely Meditation*, 'Schopenhauer as Educator': the break with Wagner is implied by the internal logic of this development. Nonetheless, there is a strange ambiguity in Nietzsche's having pretended that Cosima and Wagner would calmly accept his metamorphosis.

Nietzsche's war against Wagner and the Wagnerian movement (and against antisemitism) is a capital fact in the history of German culture, whose implications have not yet been fully recognized. Yet we should not take Nietzsche literally when he speaks, some ten years after the break, of his disappointment in Bayreuth, of the gruesome spectacle of a Wagner become old and 'rotten' and 'sinking to his knees before the Cross',[34] since Wagner had let Nietzsche know who he was from the very first day they met, and because Nietzsche himself is on record as having demonstrated his knowledge of all of Wagner's weaknesses as such beginning in 1874. However, judging from earlier examples of reticence and evasion in Wagner's presence, particularly from 1873 onward, the insight may have come some time before that.

33 Letter of Richard Wagner, beginning of January, 1872; letter of Richard Wagner, 21 September 1873.

34 *Human, All Too Human*, II, Preface, 3.

Understanding Nietzsche's attitude toward Wagner thus requires that we reject the thesis of the 'disappointment of Bayreuth', except, perhaps, in the sense that Nietzsche felt disappointed in himself before he felt disappointed in Wagner. This suffices to explain this key episode in Nietzsche's life.

The distorted accounts of these events by the Wagnerian school (such as the monograph on Wagner, cited above, of the ex-Nazi Curt von Westernhagen), which seek the reasons for Nietzsche's 'treachery' in low personal motives, are as little to the point as the mythologizations of such Nietzscheans as Ernst Bertram, according to whom Nietzsche 'betrayed' Wagner out of love, as Judas Iscariot betrayed Jesus.[35] It would be strange if the meeting of two people with such strong personalities and such different characters – Nietzsche the introvert, prisoner of his 'pathos of distance'; Wagner the extrovert, jovial and with a tendency to 'let himself go' that could easily wound his younger friend – had not produced frictions and contrasts, especially once the 'Tribschen idyll' was over and Wagner left Switzerland for Bayreuth. But the reason why Nietzsche distanced himself from Wagner is not to be sought in the personal sphere; indeed, for Nietzsche their personal encounter at Tribschen always remained the 'happiest' moment of his life. The simple and sorrowful words he wrote two years later from Marienbad to Peter Gast on 20 August 1880 are preferable to Bertram's myth and the flowery explanations of Nietzsche's sister: 'For my part, I suffer terribly when I must do without sympathy; and nothing, for instance, can compensate for the fact that I have lost Wagner's sympathy in recent years. I dream of him so often, and always in the style of the time we spent together in a relationship of

35 Ernst Bertram, *Nietzsche. Versuch einer Mythologie* (Berlin: Bondi, 1918).

confidence! We never spoke an angry word to each other, not even in my dreams, but very many encouraging and cheerful ones, and there is perhaps nobody with whom I have laughed so much. That is now *finished* – and what is the use of being *right* about him in some respects! As if that could wipe this lost sympathy from my memory!'

6. In the summer of 1878, something occurred that Nietzsche would call, eight years later, the great 'detachment'.[36] His private notes give some sense of the import and depth of the turbulence within him, of the voices that reached him in this new solitude. We have more autobiographical notes than usual from this period (the most important ones are collected in a minuscule notebook, unknown till now, inscribed with the title *Memorabilia*). But it is only a moment: soon the need to produce, 'without which life is unbearable', induces Nietzsche to turn again from introspection to expression, to the written work.[37]

We have already had occasion to speak of his notes on childhood. Nietzsche recalls the religiosity and the games of his childhood days, the happy moments of his youth. But he thinks that his education was a failure, overwhelming him with elements alien to his character that are now 'revealing' themselves. 'I am discovering myself,' he writes.[38] His sufferings must become useful to others, like 'the execution of a criminal'.[39] He would like to 'harness his sickness to the plough'.[40] The cure for pessimism consists in the decision to 'swallow the toad', that is, the

36 *Human, All Too Human*, I, Preface, 3.
37 NF 18[8], September 1876.
38 NF 28[16], *Memorabilia*, 1878.
39 NF 28[21], 1878.
40 NF 28[30], 1878.

negativity of existence. This explains the recurrent notes on a 'toad dream', a dream stretching back to the first years in Basel and which, by chance, has been transmitted to us by one of Nietzsche's friends: 'I recently dreamed that my hand, which was resting on the table in front of me, suddenly acquired a glassy, transparent skin; I could clearly see into its bones, its tissue, the play of its muscles. Suddenly I saw a fat toad sitting on my hand and felt at the same time the irresistible urge to swallow the beast. I overcame my horrible repugnance and choked it down.'[41]

The new work that Nietzsche wanted to write was supposed to have been a settling of accounts with regard to problems of art, and in particular with respect to Wagner and the Wagnerian movement. Now his judgement on Wagner became much more radical. Wagner succeeded because he knew how to 'treat his defects as virtues'; he has 'the mentality of a dilettante', he is profoundly unjust, overestimates himself, despises criticism. His music 'cannot tell or demonstrate, but only attack, disturb . . . horrify'.[42] 'What is it Wagner expresses about our era? The mixture of crudeness and softest fragility, barbarization of the natural instincts and nervous hypersensitivity, an obsession with emotion stemming from exhaustion and from delight in exhaustion.'[43] These themes will reappear in his pamphlet on Wagner ten years later. For the moment, Nietzsche limits himself to publishing an appendix to his book for free spirits: *Assorted Opinions and Maxims*. The criticisms of Wagner become allusions, the tone is extremely calm. Goethe is ever more the ideal model of nobility of spirit, of impartial tolerance,

---

41 NF 28[42], 1878. Carl Albrecht Bernoulli, *Franz Overbeck und Friedrich Nietzsche. Eine Freundschaft*, vol. 1 (Jena: Diederichs, 1908), 72.

42 NF 28[20], 1878; NF 28[52], 1878; NF 27[29], 1878.

43 NF 27[32], 1878.

of mildness and lack of envy. In the mature Goethe's 'rejection of the tragic' Nietzsche sees a positive overcoming of tragic barbarism.[44] Schiller, however, who he (like Wagner) had loved, especially when he was writing *The Birth of Tragedy*, is now rejected for his tragic pathos and moral 'idealism'. The antiromantic campaign initiated in *Human, All Too Human I* (see especially aphorism 221), which will be a constant theme in Nietzsche's work from here on, is further developed in the *Assorted Opinions and Maxims*.

7. Nietzsche's health had worsened in the meantime: on 2 May 1879, he wrote his letter of resignation to the University of Basel, and it was accepted. Nietzsche received a pension that allowed him to continue living as a wandering fugitive between France and Italy, Switzerland and Germany.[45] In the middle of June, he travelled to St Moritz in the Upper Engadine, and settled down there for three months. Discovering the landscape of the Engadine filled him with joy: 'There are certain natural landscapes in which, with a pleasurable shiver, we rediscover ourselves: it is the most beautiful way of doubling oneself.'[46] Other aphorisms in *The Wanderer and His Shadow*, the work arising in those three months, express the state of mind of the 'heroic idyll' (aph. 295) that Nietzsche experienced in the Upper Engadine.

Despite serious relapses, Nietzsche was able to enjoy good days at St Moritz and to take his long walks through the forests at the foot of the glaciers and along the edges of the small lakes. On these walks he always carried a small notebook in which he entered his thoughts in pencil. Afterwards, at home, he would

44 NF 29[1] and 29[15], 1878.

45 Cf. letter to Paul Rée, end of July 1879.

46 *The Wanderer and His Shadow*, aph. 338.

try to decipher these notes and reconstruct the reasoning, fixing it in a few essential or typical sentences. Often enough this was not successful. He would then transcribe the deciphered and reordered thoughts with pen and ink, developing and improving them and polishing their style. By the end of August, Nietzsche had filled six small notebooks. This is how *The Wanderer and His Shadow* was born, as the second and final appendix of the book for 'free spirits'.

The themes are still the same ones as in *Human, All Too Human*, but the book gives a more unified impression. In the *Assorted Opinions and Maxims* Nietzsche had, in fact, made use of formerly unused material dating back to 1875, but *The Wanderer and His Shadow* was completed over the course of just over two months.

The philosopher of *The Wanderer and His Shadow* is Epicurus, 'the soul-tamer of late antiquity' (aph. 7). The 'very closest things' must needs be the essay's object of meditation: the proper subdivision of the day, 'eating, dwelling, getting dressed, being sociable'. This is because the thoughtlessness with which we violate or ignore the most basic laws of the body and of the spirit produces 'a shameful dependency and lack of liberty . . . that fundamentally superfluous dependence on doctors, teachers and ministers' (aph. 5). Moral determinism is emphasized even more strongly ("The doctrine of the freedom of the will is an invention of the ruling classes,' aph. 9). 'Punitive' justice is criticized at length. The morality of 'reason' is contrasted with that of compassion (aph. 45), which Nietzsche rejects as harmful. *The Wanderer and His Shadow* also includes a notorious series of judgements on the major protagonists of German literature: The Germans 'were too quick to leave the school of the French – and, later, the French were too quick to enter the school of the Germans' (aph. 94). Jean Paul is 'a calamity in a dressing gown' (aph. 99). Lessing was the writer who 'studied most diligently in the French school' (aph. 103). 'Wieland wrote German better than anyone else . . . but his thoughts give us nothing further to think about' (aph. 107). 'In the history of the Germans, Goethe is an incident without consequences' (aph. 125). 'The treasury of German prose: Lichtenberg's aphorisms, the first book of Jung-Stilling's autobiography, Adalbert Stifter's *Indian Summer* and Gottfried Keller's *People of Seldwyla*', but, above all, Goethe's conversations with Eckermann (aph. 109). 'It was Herder's misfortune that his writings were always either too new or past date' (aph. 125). There are brief portraits of all the most significant German composers, while the reckoning with Wagner continues in the form of allusions: 'This most modern music, with its strong lungs and weak nerves, is always frightened first of all of itself' (aph. 166). The 'European' books closest to the Greeks are those of the French moralists: Montaigne, La Rochefoucauld, La Bruyère, Fontenelle, Vauvenargues and Chamfort – Plato would certainly have understood them, but he would have understood nothing of the major German authors, aside from Schopenhauer and Goethe, of whom he still would have understood little (aph. 214). Nietzsche's attack on 'German virtue' (aph. 216), one of the typical myths of the German nationalism originating in the wars against Napoleon, intensifies in its ironic ferocity. In his political reflections, Nietzsche comes out as a democrat and a pacifist, if in his own way: democracy is 'a necessary quarantine' to avoid tyranny (aph. 289), while political suffrage must be denied both to those without property and to the rich (aph. 293): 'Both those who own too much and those who own nothing should be regarded as public dangers' (aph. 285). As for the problem of peace and war, Nietzsche dreams of the day when the strongest and best fortified nation will voluntarily break its sword (aph. 284).

Nietzsche spends the autumn of 1879 in Naumburg with his mother. In the middle of December, Rohde, having received a copy of *The Wanderer and His Shadow*, writes to his friend: 'The conclusion of your book tears through one's soul: softer chords should and must follow this wrenching disharmony . . . You are always the one who gives, I am always the one who receives: what could I give you and be for you? if not your friend, who remains devoted and committed to you, come what may.' Nietzsche answers on 28 December: 'the magnificent testimony of your loyalty has totally shaken me'. Paul Rée received his friend's new work with enthusiasm and visited him at the end of January 1880. Meanwhile, Nietzsche had gone through a major crisis. The winter of 1879/80 was one of the most difficult of his life. This is how Nietzsche described the crisis year 1879 to the doctor Otto Eiser, in Frankfurt: 'Constant pain, for several hours each day a feeling of semi-lameness closely related to seasickness, making it difficult to speak, for variety's sake convulsive fits (the last one made me vomit for 3 days and nights, I yearned for death)'.[47] 'I had 118 days of *serious* attacks; I didn't count the lighter ones. If I could only describe to you the *continuous quality* of my condition, the constant pain and pressure in my head, on my eyes, and the overall feeling of lameness from my head to my toes!'[48]

47 Letter to Otto Eiser, beginning of January 1880.

48 Letter to Otto Eiser, middle of January 1880.

3

The Philosophy of Zarathustra (1880–84)

1. In the winter of 1880–81, during his first long stay in Genoa, Nietzsche gave definitive form to the scattered thoughts he had written down in the course of the year 1880 between Naumburg and Riva del Garda, Venice and Marienbad, then again in Naumburg and Stresa: the first year of 'roaming about' after having retired from the university. These months in a cold Genoese mansard were a time of great solitude and concentration. The pathos of this period is expressed principally in what Nietzsche called the 'new passion' (*Passio nova* appears repeatedly in the preparatory notes for *Daybreak* as a possible title for the new work): that is, the 'passion of knowledge'. If *Human, All Too Human* celebrates the liberation of the spirit, *Daybreak* is a hymn to the passion of knowledge. There is some affinity and continuity between the two moments, but, while *Human, All Too Human* is still 'the monument of a crisis',[1] that is to say, the expression of the irreparable break with the decadent, aestheticizing ideals that Nietzsche will associate from now on with the names Wagner and Schopenhauer, *Daybreak* shows a Nietzsche who has taken yet more solid possession of himself and has discovered his mission: 'In us knowledge has been transformed into a passion which shrinks at no sacrifice and at bottom fears nothing but its own extinction . . . Yes, we hate barbarism – we

1 *Ecce Homo*, 'Human, All Too Human', 1.

would all prefer the destruction of mankind to a regression of knowledge!' (aph. 429). This passion could even 'drive mankind to the point of dying with the light of an anticipatory wisdom in its eyes' (aph. 45).

Already the tone of the aphorisms dedicated to the passion of knowledge and also that of the numerous posthumous fragments in which Nietzsche pursues this theme is substantially different from the measuredness, the 'Epicurean' restraint, of the three books for free spirits which culminate in the philosophy of the 'closest things' enunciated in *The Wanderer and His Shadow* (aph. 5). Also, the longed-for community of free spirits, that lay fraternity made up of anti-metaphysical, enlightened brothers, is no longer the ideal of a Nietzsche who seems to have discovered solitude as an indispensable condition of his philosophy. This philosophy now turns to deepening the cognitive gains of the era of *Human, All Too Human*. The sober disenchantment typical of all of Nietzsche's production in the spirit of the Enlightenment or of Voltaire makes way for the new pathos, which however will never again be characterized by the unpleasant pedagogical and reform-minded intolerance of the Wagnerian period, being rooted instead in the motto of the free spirit that 'convictions are worse enemies of the truth than are lies'.[2] Nietzsche does not have any convictions, no project of reform to impose on his contemporaries; he absolutely refuses to preach to his own era. Having escaped from the prison of convictions, he has no desire to construct a new one. On the contrary, he further radicalizes the destruction of convictions: after the metaphysics of genius and of art, after the privileged experiences of religiosity, he now turns to mercilessly examining the 'moral prejudices'. In *Daybreak*, morality is stripped of every rational basis; morality, like metaphysics, falls

2 *Human, All Too Human*, I, aph. 483.

prey to history, to psychological analysis. Just as the world has no metaphysical significance, so also does it lack ethical significance, and thus – so we read in the first pages of *Daybreak* – from the historical perspective that Nietzsche assumes, the ethical significance attributed to the world ends up having the same value as the attribution of grammatical gender to the names of things (aph. 3). Like everything else that lives a long time, morality has gradually become 'so saturated with reason that [its] origin in unreason thereby becomes improbable' (aph. 1). This has allowed it to serve precisely those who could have put its rationality in question: the philosophers. Morality, Nietzsche says at the end of the path he follows in *Daybreak*, is the philosophers' Circe.[3] The philosophers have apparently striven for truth, but, in reality, they have tried to erect 'majestically moral constructions', like Kant.[4] In Nietzsche, philosophical knowledge emancipates itself from service to morality, even if the passion of knowledge – or, as he will later call it, the will to truth – is rooted precisely in the development of morality, such that in the Preface to the second edition of *Daybreak* (1886) Nietzsche can describe the meaning of his work as the 'self-sublimation of morality'. The man of knowledge is the ultimate product of morality: when he does not want to go back to what he now finds superannuated and decrepit, be it 'God, virtue, truth, justice, charity', when he no longer permits himself 'bridges-of-lies [*Lügenbrücken*] to ancient ideals', he is obeying a severe law, one higher than himself: he withdraws faith in morality – 'and why? *Out of morality*!'[5] Nietzsche's critical weapon is above all that of historical analysis, the reconstruction of the genesis of moral prejudices, supported by readings in works

3 *Daybreak*, Preface, 3.

4 Ibid., 4.

5 Ibid.

of ethnology (like John Lubbock's *The Origin of Civilization and the Primitive Condition of Man*, 1875), of history (W. E. H. Lecky, 1873, 1879, 1880), of comparative zoology (A. V. Espinas, 1878/79; C. Semper, 1880), and of moral and legal history (J. J. Baumann, 1879).[6] To this he adds a moral introspection inspired by Pascal (he rereads the *Pensées* and first encounters Sainte-Beuve's *Port-Royal* in this period), but also by Stendhal's meditations on the passions and on 'force' (*Rome, Naples, and Florence*, *De l'amour*, *History of Painting in Italy*, *Racine and Shakespeare* are among the works most read by Nietzsche at this point). Also Byron's antimoralism, which expresses itself in his pride in not being 'the slave of any appetite', draws Nietzsche's attention to manifestations of the 'moral' sphere that are grounded on the original phenomenon of a 'sense of power'.[7] And beside Byron stands Napoleon. A memoir of Napoleon by Madame de Rémusat, published in Paris in 1880, provides Nietzsche with the occasion to delineate in his notebooks a complex phenomenology of

---

6 John Lubbock, *Die Entstehung der Civilisation und der Urzustand des Menschengeschlechtes* (Jena: Costenoble, 1875) [NL]; William Edward Hartpole Lecky, *Geschichte des Ursprungs und Einflusses der Aufklärung in Europa*, trans. H. Jolowicz, 2 vols (Leipzig-Heidelberg: Winter, 1873) [NL], *Sittengeschichte Europas von Augustus bis auf Karl den Großen*, trans. H. Jolowicz, 2 vols (Leipzig-Heidelberg: Winter, 1879) [NL], *Entstehungsgeschichte-Charakteristik des Methodismus*, trans. F. Lowe (Leipzig-Heidelberg: Winter, 1880) [NL]; Alfred Vietar Espinas, *Des sociétés animales, étude de psychologie comparée* (Paris: Baillière, 1878), German translation, *Die thierischen Gesellschaften. Eine vergleichend-psychologische Untersuchung*, ed. W. Schloesser (Braunschweig: F. Vieweg und Söhne, 1879) [NL]; Karl Semper, *Die natürlichen Existenzbedingungen der Thiere* (Leipzig: Brockhaus, 1880) [NL]; Johann Julius Baumann, *Handbuch der Moral nebst Abriss der Rechtsphilosophie* (Leipzig: Hirzel, 1879) [NL].

7 *Daybreak*, aph. 109.

power.[8] These notes do not convey Nietzsche's judgement on Napoleon; he simply registers with care all the manifestations of the incarnation of the 'sense of power' (Nietzsche would later say 'will to power') that Napoleon was. And, just as Napoleon subordinated everything to the 'passion to dominate', so is it also with everyone: there is nothing more to say about the causality of so-called moral (or immoral) actions than that one instinct comes to dominate the others. Nietzsche transposes the phenomenality of the outside world ('external things are not what they appear to us to be') onto the inside world ('actions are *never* what they appear to us to be').[9] But this is not why he resolves to stop proposing moral hypotheses. Above all, Nietzsche denies that 'moral progress consists in the altruistic instincts gaining dominance over the egotistical ones, or, similarly, in the dominance of universal judgements over individual ones'.[10] On the contrary, the individual must defend 'his interests, properly understood, against other individuals', while judgements become ever more individual and universal judgements become, by contrast, ever more superficial and schematic. 'The common and *equal* person is desired only because weak people fear the strong individual and prefer a *general weakening* to the development of individuality. In today's morality I see the justification of general weakening, just as Christianity wanted to weaken and equalize the strong and spiritual people. *The tendency of altruistic morality is the smooth porridge, the soft sand of humanity*. The tendency of *universal* judgements is the commonality of feelings, that is, their poverty and exhaustion. It is the tendency toward the end of humanity.

8 Madame de Rémusat, *Mémoires 1802–1808*, 3 vols (Paris: Calmann-Lévy, 1880) [NL].

9 *Daybreak*, aph. 116.

10 NF 6[163], 1880.

The "absolute truths" are the instrument of levelling, they corrode and destroy the characteristic forms', writes Nietzsche in fragment 6[163] in the autumn of 1880, which he will then elaborate in *Daybreak* (aphs. 132 and 174). The defence of the individual in what Nietzsche calls a 'commercial society' (aph. 174) (and which we would call capitalist) is directed against the moral theories of the positivist sociologists (in particular, John Stuart Mill and Herbert Spencer) and against the attempts of the English Utilitarians to harmonize individual with social interests.

Finally, the portrait that Nietzsche draws of the apostle Paul in a long aphorism in *Daybreak* (aph. 68) is important in connection with his historical reflections on morality, supported, as we learn from contemporaneous posthumous fragments, by a deeper reading of works about the New Testament, in particular Hermann Lüdemann's *Anthropology of the Apostle Paul* (1872).[11] 'These pages of the Jewish Pascal expose the origin of Christianity as thoroughly as the pages of the French Pascal expose its destiny and that by which it will perish': specifically, the will to truth, the passion for honesty, for knowledge. Like Luther after him, Paul changed from being a zealot of the Law to being its mortal enemy, out of a conviction of being incapable of fulfilling it. The vision at Damascus means: 'it is *unreasonable* . . . to persecute precisely this Christ! For here is the way out, here is perfect revenge, here and nowhere else do I have and hold the destroyer of the law!' In fact, 'to die to evil – that means also to die to the law; to exist in the flesh – that means also to exist in the law! To become one with Christ – that means also to become with him the destroyer of the law; to have died with him – that means also to have died to the law!'[12] Paul is the first Christian,

11 Hermann Lüdemann, *Die Anthropologie des Apostels Paulus und ihre Stellung innerhalb seiner Heilslehre* (Kiel: Universitäts-Buchhandlung, 1872).

12 *Daybreak*, aph. 68, 66–8.

before him there were only a few Jewish sectarians. This is the path that will lead to *The Antichrist*, in autumn 1888.

None of Nietzsche's works after *Human, All Too Human*, including *Daybreak*, admits of a systematization of his thought: their most peculiarly 'Nietzschean' characteristic is that of being 'open' works, of tending more to the liberation of the spirit than to its catechism, of creating limpid 'infinite spaces' beyond the 'final horizon' (cf. Leopardi's poem 'L'infinito'). Nietzsche would treat the instinct for knowledge, still young and coarse, as a passion. But this passion carries within it the seed of death, of the end; it is inimical to the happy life of unconscious barbarism. Thus, we read in a fragment written toward the end of 1880: 'Yes, this passion will be our ruin! But that is no argument against it. Otherwise, death would be an argument against the life of the individual.'[13] At this point, Nietzsche no longer believes that knowledge kills force, kills instinct: 'It is true only that for the time being a new knowledge does not have a practiced mechanism at its disposal, much less a pleasurable passionate habit! But *all* that can grow! Even if it means waiting for trees to grow that will be *plucked* by a later generation – not by us!'[14] And further: 'It is now possible to lose the passionate interest in ourselves and turn that passion outward from ourselves, toward things (science). What do I matter! Pascal could not have said this.'[15] Finally, Nietzsche affirms: 'I want to bring matters to the point where a *heroic mood* is required to *devote oneself to science*!'[16] The 'Genoese' Nietzsche of the era of *Daybreak* compares the adventure of knowledge that he is espousing to navigating a ship for which all

13 NF 7[171], 1880.
14 NF 7[142], 1880.
15 NF 7[158], 1880.
16 NF 7[159], 1880.

destinations are possible. In the final aphorism of *Daybreak*, the 'shipwreck of the infinite' seems possible to Nietzsche, even though the book ends with a question that does not exclude the hope of new shores: 'Will it perhaps be said of us one day that we too, *steering westward, hoped to reach an India* – but that it was our fate to be wrecked against infinity? Or, my brothers. Or? –' (aph. 575). (The echo of Leopardi's poem 'L'infinito', let it be said in passing, is even more obvious in a fragment of autumn 1880: 'Infinity! How beautiful it is to be "shipwrecked in this sea".'[17])

After publishing *Daybreak*, in the summer of 1881 Nietzsche returned to the Engadine, but this time not to St Moritz, as in 1879, but to Sils-Maria, which (excepting in 1882) would become his summer residence until 1888. For Nietzsche, the summer of 1881 in the Engadine was rich in philosophical meditations and intuitions. Reading Spinoza (or, rather, Kuno Fischer on Spinoza), he felt he had found a predecessor, writing to Overbeck at the end of July: 'I hardly knew Spinoza: it was a matter of "acting by instinct" that I felt a need for him *now*. It's not just that his overall tendency is the same as mine – making knowledge the *strongest affect* – I recognize myself in five major points. This most abnormal and solitary thinker is closest to me in *these* things: he denies freedom of the will – ; ends – ; the moral order of the world – ; altruism – ; evil – ; there are certainly enormous differences, but these have more to do with differences of time, culture, science.'[18] The letters to Overbeck also bear evidence of the serious ailments from which Nietzsche was suffering in this period: his attacks (which could last up to three days, with atrocious headaches and

17 NF 6[364], 1880.

18 Kuno Fischer, *Geschichte der neueren Philosophie*, vol. I, part 2: *Descartes' Schule, Geulinx, Malebranche, Baruch Spinoza*. Second revised edition (Munich: Wassermann, 1865) [NL].

vomiting) alternating with periods of euphoria and of intellectual creativity. On 1 August – '6,000 feet above the sea and much higher than that above all things human!' – Nietzsche wrote in his notebook (where we also find extracts from Spinoza) a philosophical thought that would profoundly determine the entire course of his further meditations and of his works: the idea of the 'eternal recurrence of the same'. This note reads: 'The new *centre of gravity: the eternal recurrence of the same*. Infinite importance of our knowledge, of our errors, of our habits and ways of living, for everything in the future. What do we do with the rest of our life – we who have spent the greatest part of that life without knowing the most essential things? We dedicate ourselves to *teaching this doctrine* – it is the most efficient way to *assimilate* it ourselves.'[19] Teaching the doctrine of eternal recurrence will be Zarathustra's mission two years later, but the figure of the wise Persian already appears this summer in conjunction with Nietzsche's notes on this doctrine:

> This life as you now live it and have lived it you will have to live once more and innumerable times again; and there will be nothing new in it, but every pain and every joy and every thought and sigh and everything unspeakably small or great in your life must return to you, all in the same succession and sequence – even this spider and this moonlight between the trees, and even this moment and I myself. The eternal hourglass of existence is turned over and over again, and you with it, speck of dust![20]

19 NF 11[141], 1881.

20 *The Gay Science: With a Prelude in Rhymes and an Appendix of Songs*, edited by Bernard Williams, translated by Josefine Nauckhoff, poems translated by Adrian Del Caro (Cambridge: Cambridge University Press, 2001), aph. 341, 194 [hereinafter GS].

Aside from the posthumous fragments, this is the most explicit of Nietzsche's few descriptions of 'eternal recurrence'.

During his second stay in Genoa (winter 1881–82), Nietzsche initially meant to continue the work he had published the year before, and under the title *Continuation of 'Daybreak'* he transcribed a large part of the thoughts he had been accumulating in his notebooks, excepting the ones dedicated to the eternal recurrence of the same.[21] This was the origin of *The Gay Science*. In the definitive edition, this comprises five books. Four of these were published by Nietzsche in the summer of 1882, with the verse prelude 'Joke, Cunning and Revenge'. The first book's recurrent theme is that of the importance of 'evil' in human history: 'all ethical systems hitherto have been so foolish and contrary to nature that humanity would have perished from every one had it gained power over humanity' (aph. 1, GS 28–9). The second book is mostly devoted to questions of art, understood as 'the good will to appearance', as a means of supporting 'the general untruth and mendacity' promoted by science and of resting from the weight of ourselves (aph. 107, GS 104). The third could be called the book of the 'death of God': 'We have killed him! . . . and whoever is born after us will on account of this deed belong to a higher history than all history up to now!' (aph. 125, GS 120). The fourth book, 'Sanctus Januarius' (a 'very special memorial to one of [his] last winters in the South', as Jacob Burckhardt wrote in a letter to Nietzsche of 13 September 1882), reflects Nietzsche's new state of mind: the end of the book announces 'Zarathustra's going under', the hermit's descent among humankind.

2. *The Gay Science* prepares for Nietzsche the work in which he intends to announce his philosophy of the affirmation of life.

21 NF 16[1], 1881/82.

Nietzsche had been seeking a new form of expression for some time, since at least August 1881. Zarathustra was already the protagonist of many aphorisms in *The Gay Science*. Yet we have no coherent draft of the deeds and sayings of Zarathustra, only scattered hints in the notebooks of 1881–82, and titles like 'Midday and Eternity' and 'Zarathustra's Idleness', all going back to autumn 1881. A key aphorism of *The Gay Science* (125, on the 'death of God') has Zarathustra as its protagonist; in the final draft, the name of the Persian sage is replaced with 'the crazy man'. Despite the significant mass of posthumous notes from this period, it is impossible to reconstruct how Nietzsche reworked this aphorism to yield the version in verse of *Thus Spoke Zarathustra* (Preface, 1). Thus, for instance, in aphorism 342 of *The Gay Science* the name Zarathustra directly follows the sketch of the 'eternal recurrence of the same' in aphorism 341, but it is not clear why Nietzsche mentions it at this juncture. The reason for this choice later given in *Ecce Homo* sounds like a justification *a posteriori*, required in the context of the writings planned in the autumn of 1888 (especially *The Immoralist*).[22]

An aphorism in *The Gay Science* casts some light on the reasons why Nietzsche moved from the compact form of the aphorism to the compositional freedom of Zarathustra's 'discourses': 'Must not he who wants to move the crowd be an actor playing the role of himself? Must he not first translate himself into the grotesquely obvious and *present* his entire person and cause in this coarsened and simplified version?' (aph. 236, GS 147). The preparatory note for this aphorism reads: 'If Zarathustra would move the multitudes, he must be an actor who impersonates himself.'[23] The fact that Nietzsche waited to introduce the figure of Zarathustra, eliminating him from all the aphorisms in traditional

22 *Ecce Homo*, 'Why I Am a Destiny', 3.

23 NF 12[112], 1881.

form and presenting him only in the final aphorism of *The Gay Science* (in the first edition of 1882), which is nearly identical to the beginning of *Thus Spoke Zarathustra*, suggests that the choice of this form of expression reached maturity with this aphorism, which foreshadows *Zarathustra*. The manuscripts also show that this aphorism was not only numerically the last in the book, but also that it was the last one Nietzsche wrote.

But, as we shall see, the real problem of *Zarathustra*'s form of expression is closely linked with a sort of difficulty, or indeed the impossibility, of Nietzsche's expressing himself 'as a poet', as well as with his condemnation of poetry as something opposed to truth. 'Poetry and truth': what was still possible for Goethe is no longer so for Nietzsche. In the fourth part of *Zarathustra* the 'Mage' (in whom we can recognize traits of Wagner) laments, in his 'Song of Melancholy', that he is 'banished / From all truth, / Only fool! / Only poet!' Before putting it into the mouth of the mage-actor-Wagner, Nietzsche had written this poem for himself, in a series of poetic sketches bearing the title *The Poet – Torment of the Creator*.[24] In this torment, Nietzsche once again recognizes his affinity but also his antagonism with Wagner, who was a poet, an artist, indeed an actor, all in good conscience.

3. To understand the pathos of Zarathustra, we must not forget that his purpose for Nietzsche was to preach the doctrine of the 'eternal recurrence of the same', and that all of his 'Thou shalts' are thus illuminated and transfigured by the new light of this 'knowledge'. Karl Löwith may be credited with having indicated the centrality of this doctrine to all Nietzsche's thinking.[25] We do

24 NF 28[27], 1884.

25 Karl Löwith, *Nietzsches Philosophie der ewigen Wiederkehr des Gleichen* (Stuttgart: Kohlhammer, 1956).

not accept his attempt to establish a coherent line of development from the youthful essay 'Fate and History' (1862) all the way to the fragments of the so-called *Will To Power*, with which Löwith means to demonstrate the systematic nature of Nietzsche's thought; but we agree with him that the idea of the 'eternal recurrence of the same' was *the culminating event in Nietzsche's life*. We must for this reason return to those first days of August 1881 in which Nietzsche first experienced this idea as an absolutely new and overwhelming truth.

We have cited the aphorism in *The Gay Science* in which Nietzsche first expounded the notion of eternal recurrence, without defining it as such. The letters of August 1881 express euphoria, but also, inevitably, despondence. Nietzsche had suffered a great deal that summer. 'Sum in puncto *desperationis*. Dolor vincit vitam voluntatemque. O quos menses, qualem aestatem habui!' he writes on 18 September 1881 to Overbeck.[26] It is in this condition that he comes up with the idea of eternal recurrence.

The anthroposophist Rudolf Steiner has observed that Nietzsche must have read something comparable in Eugen Dühring's *Course of Philosophy* (1875), and Lou Andreas-Salomé notes that, in the second *Untimely Meditation*, on history, Nietzsche himself had attributed a similar theory to the Pythagoreans, while, in general, a 'cyclical' conception of eternity was widespread in classical antiquity.[27] Henri Lichtenberger and Charles Andler have pointed to three works, more or less contemporary with Nietzsche, in

---

26 'I am at the point of *despair*. Pain overcomes life and will. Oh, what months, what a summer I have had! '

27 Rudolph Steiner, *Friedrich Nietzsche. Ein Kämpfer gegen seine Zeit* (Weimar: Felber, 1895); Karl Eugen Dühring, *Cursus der Philosophie als streng wissenschaftlicher Weltanschauung und Lebensgestaltung* (Leipzig: E. Koschny, 1875) [NL]; Lou Andreas-Salomé, *Friedrich Nietzsche in seinen Werken* (Vienna: Konegen, 1894).

which the same theory, or at least the same hypothesis, can be found: Johannes Gustav Vogt, *Force: A Real-Monistic Worldview* (1878); Louis-Auguste Blanqui, *Eternity Through the Stars* (1872); and Gustave Le Bon, *Man and Society* (1881).[28] We find no trace of the last-named work in Nietzsche's manuscripts. However, Nietzsche did read Vogt's book at Sils-Maria in the summer of 1881. A fragment from this period (to which Andler rightly calls attention) reads: 'He who does not believe in a *cyclical process of the universe* must believe in an *arbitrary* God – this is how my conception differs from all theistic conceptions to date!'[29] Nietzsche received Vogt's book from his friend Overbeck in mid-September, a month and a half before the new idea had 'risen . . . on [his] horizon'.[30] What is more important than these chronological observations is the intimate link between eternal recurrence, understood as a circular cosmic process, and the negation of the creator-god of the Christians whose death Nietzsche will announce in *The Gay Science*. The book by the Communard Louis-Auguste Blanqui is first referred to in a notebook of 1883.[31] It is more likely that Nietzsche did not yet know *Eternity Through the Stars* in 1881, and that one of his acquaintances (Gast? Malwida von Meysenbug? Overbeck?), having read *Zarathustra* or aphorism 341 of *The Gay*

28 Henri Lichtenberger, *La philosophie de Nietzsche* (Paris: Alcan, 1911), appendix; Charles Andler, *Nietzsche, sa vie et sa pensée*, 3 vols (Paris: Gallimard, 1958), vol. II, 421–2; Johannes Gustav Vogt, *Die Kraft. Eine real-monistische Weltanschauung*, vol. I: *Die Kontraktionsenergie, die letztursächliche einheitliche mechanische Wirkungsform des Weltsubstrates* (Leipzig: Haupt & Teschler, 1878) [NL]; Louis-Auguste Blanqui, *L'éternité par les astres. Hypothèse astronomique* (Paris: Baillière, 1872); Gustave Le Bon, *L'homme et les sociétés. Leurs origines et leur histoire*, 2 vols (Paris: Rothschild, 1881).

29 Cf. Vogt, *Die Kraft*, 90; NF 11[312], 1881.

30 Letter to Heinrich Köselitz, 14 August 1881.

31 NF 17[73], 1883.

Science, called his attention to Blanqui. Indeed, the similarities are surprising. The French revolutionary had written this 'poem in prose' in the prison of Fort de Taureau, where he had been incarcerated by Thiers.[32] Here he writes, for example: 'What I am writing at this moment in the Fort de Taureau, I have already written, and will write in eternity, at a table, with a pen, wearing these clothes, in circumstances that are in every respect identical.'[33] The only difference is that Blanqui supposes not only a repetition in infinite time, but also a repetition in infinite space (which Nietzsche explicitly denies), with the possibility of infinite variations, not just repetitions of the same event: 'Of every being there exist identical doubles and variants of these doubles, which multiply and represent its personality in every moment, if only in fragments. Everything that one could have been here, one really is at some other point in the universe.'[34] Blanqui, like Nietzsche, was not a scientist, but the scientific hypothesis of an eternal repetition of the same did preoccupy scientists at the time, and in the months immediately following August 1881, and repeatedly in the years after that, Nietzsche made an effort to seek scientific confirmation of his 'doctrine' and to ground it scientifically himself. He found the most emphatic objections in the pseudoscience of Dühring's *Course of Philosophy*, which he took up again in 1885, as well as in a lecture of 1884 by Carl von Nägeli, a much more respectable scientist. It is curious to observe how, in the notes for his *Dialectics of Nature* (1883), Friedrich Engels – having read this lecture in the edition of 1877, whereas Nietzsche knew it from an edition of 1884 – objects to Nägeli's assertion that the Infinite is incomprehensible: 'When we say that material and motion are not created and are

32 Lichtenberger, *La philosophie de Nietzsche*.

33 Blanqui, *L'éternité par les astres*, 73.

34 Ibid., 57.

indestructible, we are saying that they exist as infinite progress, i.e. in the form of bad infinity, and with that we have understood everything there is to understand about this process. All that is left is to ask if this process is an eternal repetition of the same – in large cycles – or whether the cycles have descending and ascending ramifications.'[35] In short – as Lichtenberger has already observed – Nietzsche's most paradoxical theory was born of a scientific hypothesis that enjoyed great popularity at the time. Naturally, Nietzsche was aware that he was dealing with a hypothesis, but – somewhat like Pascal – he wrote: 'Even if cyclical repetition is merely a probability or a possibility, still the *thought of a possibility* can unsettle and transform us . . . ! What an effect the thought of eternal damnation has had!'[36] Precisely here we discern one of the grounds for Nietzsche's decision to have Zarathustra 'preach' eternal recurrence. In the final analysis, if knowledge is always the 'radical misunderstanding of existence' and error 'the condition of life', then the great reformers, like Mohammed – so Nietzsche argues (as Zarathustra-Nietzsche, we would add) – were not calling on people to strive after 'something else', but, rather, 'to see what they *want to have and can have* as something higher (to "discover" more reason and happiness therein than they have found up to now)'.[37] The fact that the hypothesis of the eternal recurrence of the same can be found so to speak at the outer limit of scientific knowledge, that it could in fact be the necessary corollary of a rigidly deterministic and thoroughly 'atheistic' conception of existence, satisfies Nietzsche's 'passion of knowledge'. Nietzsche wants however to reform humanity – 'there will arise a

35 Karl Marx and Friedrich Engels, *Werke*, vol. 20 (Berlin: Dietz Verlag, 1972), 503–4.

36 NF 11[203], 1881.

37 NF 11[162], 1881; NF 11[19], 1881.

universal terrestrial man' – for 'in the long run even a simple hypothesis can be stronger than a belief, provided it subsists much longer than a religious dogma'.[38] This is Zarathustra's 'Machiavellianism', for which Nietzsche moreover leaves a great deal of time: 'Let us guard against teaching such a doctrine like a religion! . . . What are the couple of millennia in which Christianity has sustained itself! The mightiest idea requires many millennia – it must be small and impotent *for a long, long time*!'[39] This 'mightiest idea' is evidently a close neighbour to religion, even if it is, in fact, the end of all religion and a negation of metaphysics even more radical than that of the free spirit.

It cannot be said with certainty that Nietzsche 'believed' in the eternal recurrence of the same. In the manuscripts, certainty alternates with doubt; in *Zarathustra*, the theory is mostly announced in the form of symbols rather than demonstrated. In any case, it may be interesting to quote what seems the most convincing of the 'proofs' that we find in the manuscripts:

> The world of forces suffers no diminution: otherwise, over the course of eternal time it would have become weak and would have perished. The world of forces suffers no stasis: otherwise, this would have been attained, and the clock of being would have come to a halt. The world of forces thus never achieves an equilibrium, it never enjoys a moment of calm, its force and its movement are equally great at all times. Whatever state this world *can* attain, it must have attained, and not only once, but countless times. This moment, for example: it has already been here, and many times, and it will likewise recur, with all its forces distributed just as they are now; and it is the same with

38 NF 11[274], 1881; NF 11[248], 1881.

39 NF 11[158], 1881.

> the moment that bore this one, and with the moment that is the child of the present moment.

Here, it becomes apparent that the conception of infinite time means the negation of becoming and the eternalization of the moment: 'everything is eternal, it has not become'.[40] To describe the eternal cycle there is 'no need to revert to the flawed analogy of cycles of emergence and decay, such as for example the stars or ebb and flood, day and night, the seasons'.[41] Nietzsche repeats these arguments multiple times, without ever arriving at a formulation that corresponds to the conviction with which he describes *the consequences* of the 'mightiest idea'. He thus contents himself with the (rational) 'probability' of his theory and turns to the individual with the command to live 'such that we might want to live the same life again, and to live that way throughout all eternity!'[42] The difference between those who believe in eternal recurrence and those who do not is that the former confer on their lives the imprint of eternity, whereas the latter live a 'fleeting life'.[43] The individual must shape his life like a work of art, and, in this, he will be helped precisely by the belief that he will relive this life eternally. Eternal recurrence thus also means the end of any form of teleology: the universe has neither moral nor aesthetic purpose, the cycle of becoming is innocent. This, however, permits what Nietzsche calls the 'dehumanization of nature' and the assimilation of all the experiences of the past, of all human good and evil, of all the errors that have conditioned life and which continue to condition it.[44] The

40 NF 11[148], 1881.

41 Ibid.

42 NF 11[161], 1881.

43 NF 11[160], 1881.

44 NF 11[197], 1881.

culmination of this new 'great cosmodicy' is symbolized by the '*annulus aeternitatis*':[45] 'The sun of knowledge stands once again at noon, and the snake of eternity lies coiled in its light – this is your time, you brothers of the meridian!'[46]

4. Everything we have been discussing goes back to the spring and autumn of 1881. The notes of this period include no reference at all to another important idea, the linchpin of the second part of *Zarathustra*: the idea of the *Übermensch*, the overman. The subject of Zarathustra's first preaching is not eternal recurrence, but the overman. There is no mention of the overman in *The Gay Science*, nor any trace of the idea in the manuscripts immediately preceding the fair copy of the first part of *Thus Spoke Zarathustra*. We can thus place its origin in the winter of 1882–83, the winter in which Nietzsche is at the mercy of grave psychic suffering, breaks with his family and is tormented by resentment of Lou and Rée and even more of himself, a winter 'on the verge of suicide'. This was the winter in which the overman was born.

In December 1882, at the high point of the crisis, Nietzsche writes in a private note: 'I do not want life *again*. How have I managed to bear it? Producing. What allows me to bear the moment? The vision of the overman, of him who *says yes* to life. I myself have tried to say yes to it – ach!'[47] Thus Nietzsche is not the overman; the overman is nothing other than the person who is able to say yes to life as it is, in eternal repetition. This is what links the theory of eternal recurrence with the doctrine of the overman. To accept total immanence, the world after the death of God, man must raise himself above himself, he must 'go under' so

45 Ibid.

46 NF 11[196], 1881.

47 NF 4[81], 1882–83.

that the overman might be born. The 'universal terrestrial man' of 1881 now seems inadequate; only a superhuman being could bear a life that repeats eternally. The complementary concept to the overman is the 'last man': 'the most contemptible human, who can no longer have contempt for himself', who 'makes everything small'.[48] But even the last man will recur eternally. For Nietzsche, this is the most serious objection (!) to eternal recurrence. In general, it was this winter's experiences that led him to imagine a life that could not be lived as if it were to repeat throughout all eternity without being overwhelmed by nausea and crushed by despair. Through a typical process of sublimation of even his own most demoralizing experiences – 'who knows if this time as well I'll succeed in turning dirt into gold' – this 'state of emergency' produces the idea of the overman.[49] By keeping in mind, while reading *Zarathustra*, that the overman makes sense for Nietzsche *only* in relation to eternal recurrence, one can avoid gross misunderstandings and take both eternal recurrence and the overman for what they were in Nietzsche's mind: eternal recurrence is not a sort of *salto mortale* into irrationality in search of another 'world behind the world', or, worse, a bloodless surrogate for religion; the overman, precisely because of his connection with eternal recurrence, is not an aestheticizing athlete bursting with health or, worse yet, the prototype of a 'master race'.[50] Rather, both are limiting concepts at the horizon of an anti-metaphysical and anti-pessimistic vision of the world, following the 'death of God'.

5. The problems posed in *The Birth of Tragedy* and *Thus Spoke Zarathustra* are identical, or, better: the tendency of the two books

48 *Thus Spoke Zarathustra*, 'Zarathustra's Prologue', 10.

49 Letter to Franz Overbeck, 25 December 1882.

50 NF 11[163], 1881.

is the same, but the solutions, the outcomes, are opposites. Just as, in *The Birth of Tragedy*, Nietzsche tends to a general justification of existence (which is the meaning of 'saying yes to life') and achieves it in the 'metaphysics of art', in *Zarathustra* eternal recurrence, desired by the overman, nullifies the problem of justifying existence, closing off the horizon not by means of the 'tragic myth' but with the 'eternalization' of life's fundamentally terrestrial and immanent character.

As he did after *The Birth of Tragedy*, following *Zarathustra* Nietzsche attempted to work with knowledge attained at the edge of rationality. But, this time, the undertaking was more difficult, since the content of the new knowledge of eternal recurrence could not be expressed by recourse to artistic mystification, to the metaphysical creation of the 'tragic myth'. And this is the true problem of 'expression' in *Zarathustra*. While, in the era of *The Birth of Tragedy*, Nietzsche was prepared for the possibility of becoming a poet (see the letter to Rohde of 29 March 1871), Zarathustra is a poet with a 'bad conscience'. 'The poets lie too much? But Zarathustra, too, is a poet . . . But supposing that someone said in all seriousness that the poets lie too much. He would be right: *we* lie too much. We also know too little and are bad learners, thus we simply have to lie.'[51] The obsessive search for antitheses, the mode of expression overloaded with symbolism, the superabundance of similes whose monotony derives from the way they nearly all repeat the same rhetorical patterns, the constant hammering of superlatives, Zarathustra's inability to 'warm the heart' of his readers, the total absence of joy despite Zarathustra's 'dancing' and 'laughter', the unchecked wordplay – all this makes *Thus Spoke Zarathustra* the grandiose antipode of a poetic work.[52] It is a

51 *Thus Spoke Zarathustra*, Second Part, 'On Poets', 100.

52 Löwith, *Nietzsches Philosophie der ewigen Wiederkehr des Gleichen.*

grotesque mistake to seek aesthetic pleasure in *Zarathustra*, just as it is to seek in it a substitute for religion or metaphysics. Both things have occurred, but those who have let themselves be bewitched by the so-called perfection of Nietzsche's style, like those who have sought in the book satisfaction of their religious needs, have ignored the passion that dictated Nietzsche's strange 'poem' to him. This passion shatters all the bounds of poetic invention. This passion is the passion of the 'spirit' (*Geist* = mind, not *Seele* = soul), of which Nietzsche says: 'Spirit is life that itself cuts into life; by its own agony it increases its own knowledge.'[53]

Finally, the Nietzsche of *The Birth of Tragedy* was not alone, for, together with Wagner, he believed he was fighting to reform German culture, against the 'sense of an autumn of culture'.[54] The Nietzsche of *Thus Spoke Zarathustra* takes the bull by the horns in an attempt to overturn the values of existing society so as to recover an entirely terrestrial vision of man and of life. This attempt occurs in complete solitude; it is entirely individual. 'This is how I want to live: illuminated by the virtues of a world that does not yet exist', Nietzsche wrote in this winter of 1882–83.[55] *Thus Spoke Zarathustra* is also a utopia.

53 *Thus Spoke Zarathustra*, Second Part, 'On the Famous Wise Men', 80.
54 NF 28[1], 1878.
55 NF 5[1], 146, 1882.

4
The Late Nietzsche (1885–89)

1. From the winter of 1882–83 through the spring of 1888, there occurs no outward event of importance in Nietzsche's life. The march into solitude continues. In Basel, Overbeck takes care of all financial matters for his friend: he collects Nietzsche's pension, manages his small savings account, sends him money as needed. In Venice, Peter Gast helps him correct proofs and plays the part of the disciple. Nietzsche's visits to Overbeck in Basel and to Gast in Venice are the only real interruptions in his solitary life. Nietzsche regularly spends every summer, from June or July through September or October, in Sils-Maria, and most of the autumn and winter in Nice. He returns to Germany, for a few weeks each time, in September 1883, September 1885, May 1886: Naumburg, Leipzig, Monaco are the cities where he stays the longest. His relationship to his sister worsens during the summer of 1883–84 on account of her engagement to the notorious antisemite and Wagnerian Bernhard Förster. A reconciliation takes place at Zurich in the autumn of 1884. Nietzsche sees his sister again the next autumn in Naumburg, before she departs with her husband for Paraguay. The letters of 1887 and 1888 document the irreparable conflict between Nietzsche and his sister. At the end of August 1884, he receives a visit from Heinrich von Stein, a pupil of Dühring's and a Wagnerian. At the end of November, Nietzsche writes the poem 'Longings of a Hermit', in which he

expresses the hope that his friends might return to the hermit, and sends it to Stein. But Stein remains faithful to Bayreuth. In the final draft of the poem, which he will publish under the title 'From the High Mountains' at the end of *Beyond Good and Evil*, Nietzsche puts an end to the solitude and the waiting with the arrival of . . . Zarathustra. A few female acquaintances are no more than minor characters in Nietzsche's life during these years: Resa von Schirnhofer and Meta von Salis, followed by Malwida von Meysenbug, the writer Helene Druscowitz, Schopenhauer's English translator Helen Zimmern, and other women staying at Nice and Sils-Maria. During his stay at Nice in 1883–84, a kind of friendship develops with Paul Lanzky, an obscure German poet and the co-owner of a hotel in Vallombrosa. As Erich F. Podach was the first to observe, an encounter, lasting a couple of weeks, with the young Viennese doctor Joseph Paneth is of interest because it established a kind of connection between Nietzsche and psychoanalysis.[1] Paneth is indeed none other than the 'friend Joseph' mentioned by Freud in *The Interpretation of Dreams*. Paneth described his encounters with Nietzsche in an extremely interesting diary;[2] he is also a witness to Nietzsche's still subterranean influence during these years. It is thus quite likely that Freud knew of Nietzsche and his ideas fairly early on, through Paneth. A meeting with Gottfried Keller in Zurich in October 1884 and a short exchange of letters with Hippolyte Taine begun in 1886 close out the list of Nietzsche's life events in this period.

Nietzsche has no human relationships that could be compared to his friendship with Rohde during the Leipzig and Basel years,

---

1 Erich F. Podach, *Ein Blick in Notizbücher Nietzsches* (Heidelberg: Rothe, 1963), 185.

2 Published whole in KGW VII/4.2, 9–28.

or with the 'brotherhood in arms' enjoyed with Overbeck while writing the *Untimely Meditations*, or – still less – with the 'Tribschen idyll' shared with Cosima and Richard Wagner, or with his passionate exchange of ideas with Paul Rée.

Nietzsche had a final encounter with Rohde in Leipzig in the spring of 1886, but this meeting confirmed the estrangement that had arisen over the course of the last eight years. A few months later, Nietzsche wrote a letter (21 May 1887) deepening the breach between them on the flimsy pretext of their differing opinions on Taine.

On his last meeting with Nietzsche, Rohde wrote to Overbeck: 'An indescribable atmosphere of *strangeness*, something that felt absolutely *uncanny* to me, surrounded him. There was something in him that I did not recognize, and a lot was no longer there that used to characterize him. Like he was coming from a country where nobody else was living.'[3]

The four parts of *Thus Spoke Zarathustra* appeared one after another between 1883 and 1885. In 1886 and 1887, Nietzsche published new prefaces to *The Birth of Tragedy*, to the two volumes of *Human, All Too Human* (the two appendices of 1878–79 make up the second volume), to *Daybreak* and *The Gay Science* (to which he adds a fifth book and the 'Songs of Prince Vogelfrei'). As new works – published at his own expense, since, following part four of *Zarathustra*, he no longer had a publisher willing to risk printing his writings – there appeared *Beyond Good and Evil: Prelude to a Philosophy of the Future* and *On the Genealogy of Morality*. If we count up all the pages published between 1883 and 1887, we have about a thousand printed pages, while the unpublished manuscript material from the same period amounts to at

3 24 January 1889, in Andreas Patzer, ed., *Franz Overbeck–Erwin Rohde. Briefwechsel. Supplementa Nietzscheana l* (Berlin: de Gruyter, 1990), 135.

least 1,500 pages, not counting the manuscripts probably lost, such as those from the period of the *Genealogy of Morality* (1887).

Nietzsche dedicates himself ever more intensely to the only activity that allows him 'to endure life': writing. After publishing *Zarathustra*, his plans oscillate. Initially he believes he has written the 'yea-saying part' of his philosophy, and that it is now time to expound the negative, 'nay-saying, *nay-doing* part'.[4] All the material accumulated while writing *Zarathustra* must be used to develop a critique of morality, the theory of knowledge, of aesthetics, etc. *Beyond Good and Evil* is made up mainly of material collected between 1883 and 1885. But if this work is the 'prelude to a philosophy of the future' and if on the other hand it 'says the same thing as . . . *Zarathustra*, only in a different way', then *Thus Spoke Zarathustra* is also merely a prelude, and, in fact, Nietzsche describes it as the 'vestibule' (*Vorhalle*) to his philosophy.[5] Where, then, do we find the philosophy itself? In the summer of 1886, the back cover of *Beyond Good and Evil* expressly announces the 'philosophy of the future' with the title and subtitle: *The Will to Power. Attempt at a Transvaluation of All Values.*

2. We must now attend particularly to the problem of the 'will to power', which dominates Nietzsche's late work. The phrase 'will to power' refers, in the first place, to a philosophical idea of Nietzsche's, in the second to a literary project of his. The definition of the will to power, already adumbrated in reflections of 1880 on the 'sense of power' in *Daybreak* and in posthumous fragments from the same period, is developed in the second half of *Thus Spoke Zarathustra*, in the chapter 'On Self-Overcoming':

---

4 *Ecce Homo*, 'Beyond Good and Evil', 1.

5 Letter to Jacob Burckhardt, 22 September 1886.

> Wherever I found the living, there I found will to power . . . And life itself spoke this secret to me: 'Behold,' it said, 'I am *that which must always overcome itself* . . . And even you, seeker of knowledge, are only a path and footstep of my will; indeed, my will to power follows also on the heels of your will to truth! Indeed, the one who shot at truth with the words "will to existence" did not hit it: this will – does not exist! For, what *is* not can not will; but what is in existence, how could this still will to exist? Only where life is, is there also will; but not will to life, instead – thus I teach you – will to power! Much is esteemed more highly by life than life itself; yet out of esteeming itself speaks – the will to power!'[6]

This description of the 'will to power' is from 1883, and it holds good for Nietzsche until the end. Let us then try to specify the essential characteristics. The will to power, the will to domination, the will to possession, are life itself; wherever there is life, there is also the will to power. This will to power is not a metaphysical principle like Schopenhauer's will to exist or to live. It does not 'manifest' itself, but is simply another word for life, another way of defining life. For Nietzsche life is the relationship of stronger and weaker, but, above all, the will of everything living to overcome itself, the will of the living being that puts itself at risk 'for the love of power'. And the will to truth (which Nietzsche, beginning with *Daybreak*, had earlier called the 'passion for knowledge') is also a will to power, a 'will to render all being thinkable' and thus make it 'behave and bend' to the will of the wisest ones, and 'become smooth and subservient to the spirit, as its mirror and reflection'. 'What the people believe to be

6 *Thus Spoke Zarathustra*, Second Part, 'On Self-Overcoming', 89–90 [translation modified].

good and evil' reveals the will to power of the creators of values, of those who bestowed a heritage of moral beliefs upon what Nietzsche calls the 'people' (*das Volk*).[7]

Having recalled to mind, albeit summarily, what Nietzsche meant by the expression 'will to power', let us turn our attention to his literary project of writing a work with the title *The Will to Power*. This title first appears in Nietzsche's manuscripts of late summer 1885. This is preceded by a series of notes that can be dated to spring of the same year. To keep things in proper perspective, we would emphasize that the theme of the 'will to power' is just one of many ideas rehearsed in the posthumous fragments and that the title, too – when it is used for the first time – is not the only one Nietzsche orients his thinking on. The historical sense, consciousness as a falsification that makes life possible, the critique of modern moral *tartufferie*, the definition of the philosopher as legislator and experimenter with new possibilities, the so-called 'great politics', the characterization of the good European: we find all these motifs and more in the notebooks and copy-books of this period. Here, too, Nietzsche's posthumous papers reveal themselves as the intellectual diary that they really were, a diary in which Nietzsche registered all his attempts at theoretical elaboration, as well as what he was reading (normally in the form of extracts), drafts of letters, and the titles of works that he wanted to write, along with the relevant plans. It is important not to lose sight of the fact that these notes are very complex experiments that can be understood only within their overall context. Of these manifold titles and plans we can say that some are titles deriving from prior notes, but also that other titles, appearing in isolation, indicate some as yet undeveloped intention, just as there are plans which are linked to notes,

7 Ibid., 88.

or to a title, or which are connected neither to surrounding notes nor with any title. What all of these have in common is the tense experimental atmosphere characteristic of the manuscripts, an atmosphere which should be taken seriously, for it resists all attempts at systematization, any 'will to system'. Thus if we provisionally isolate such a central idea as the 'will to power' and a literary project with the title *The Will to Power*, we do so only in order to facilitate discussion, and, ultimately, to demonstrate that such a procedure inevitably casts Nietzsche's work in a false light, unless one makes the effort to relativize it by setting it within the organic context of all his philosophical meditations and literary projects and understanding it as 'thought in the state of becoming'.

Let us therefore return to the fragments of spring 1885 that appear to anticipate the project of *The Will to Power* as a discrete work. In a notebook from April through June 1885, Nietzsche sets forth the hypothesis 'that it is the will to power which governs the inorganic world as well, or rather, that there *is* no inorganic world' governed by mechanistic laws.[8] Such laws might facilitate the superficial description of the outside world, but they fail to eliminate 'action at a distance', which is however the 'fundamental fact' ('*something draws something else closer, something feels drawn*'). To express itself, this will to power must 'perceive those things that it draws closer'; it must feel 'the approach of something it can assimilate'.[9] What is interesting here is not the theoretical basis of this fragment, but, rather, the fact that Nietzsche is extending the will to power to the inorganic world (in

8 NF 34[247], 1885; Friedrich Nietzsche, *Writings from the Late Notebooks*, ed. Rüdiger Bittner, trans. Kate Sturge (Cambridge: Cambridge University Press, 2003), 15 [hereinafter WLN].

9 NF 34[247], 1885; WLN, 15.

Zarathustra he had spoken only of 'living beings'). Shortly thereafter, in a notebook of May–July 1885, we find a fragment with the title 'Regarding the Plan. *Introduction*'.[10] This alludes to a plan without any working title, the first to develop the notion of a will to power in the inorganic world. The organic functions are 'translated back into the fundamental will, the will to power', and split off from it, producing 'thinking, feeling, willing in everything that lives'. The will to power also becomes specialized as a will to nourishment, to property, to tools, to servants. A system of 'obeying and mastering' governs the human body (which is for Nietzsche at this point the only guide to reality). 'The stronger will directs the weaker. There is no other causality whatsoever than that of will on will', Nietzsche says, returning to his critique of mechanistic causalism. Ultimately, even the 'intellectual functions' constitute will to power, as the will to give form (*Wille zur Gestaltung*) and the will to assimilation (*Wille zur Anähnlichung*).[11] Here, then, we have an introduction to a work that is not described in any greater detail, and the theme of this introduction is the 'will to power'. A peculiar fragment in the same notebook, unknown until now, addresses the relationship between 'will to power' and the 'person'. The fragment is titled (with reference to the theory of the eternal recurrence of the same) *On the Ring of Rings*:

> There is an *inside* to the force that changes and yet remains always the same, a sort of Proteus-Dionysus character that dissimulates and takes pleasure in change. The 'person' understood as illusion: effectively, *heredity* is the main objection, in that a great many formative forces from much earlier times

10 NF 35[15], 1885; WLN, 18.

11 Ibid.

> continue to exert themselves: in truth, these forces struggle within the person and are governed and dominated – a will to power permeates the person, it requires the *diminution* of perspectives, it requires 'egotism' as a *temporary condition of existence*; from every stage of the will to power it looks upward to a higher one. The reduction of the efficient principle to the 'person', to the individual.[12]

Here, Nietzsche seems to want to gauge the capacity of the will to power to present itself – by analogy with Schopenhauer's 'will to live' – as a thing-in-itself manifesting itself, through the *principium individuationis*, as a plurality of persons. But, despite the peremptory tone of his formulation, Nietzsche seems unconvinced by this hypothesis. What is more, these lines were crossed out with a pen, which suggests that he was not entirely satisfied with this formulation of his theory of the will to power. Let us then view this fragment as an important provisional formulation, as an attempt to resolve the problem of the relationship between the doctrine of the eternal recurrence of the same and that of the will to power. This is confirmed by the formulation of this relationship in an analogous fragment written shortly afterward. The fragment is fairly well known, for it was placed by the compilers of *The Will to Power* (the work Nietzsche never wrote, as we shall see) at the very end of their edition (note the arbitrary chronology: this fragment dates to June–July 1885, and thus from a period in which Nietzsche had not yet decided to write a work with this title). The fragment reads:

> And do you know what 'the world' is to me? Shall I show it to you in my mirror? This world: a monster of energy, without

12 NF 35[68], 1885.

beginning, without end, a fixed, iron quantity of force which grows neither larger nor smaller, which doesn't exhaust but only transforms itself, as a whole unchanging in size, an economy without expenditure and losses, but equally without increase, without income, enclosed by 'nothingness' as by a boundary; not something blurred, squandered, not something infinitely extended; instead, as a determinate force set into a determinate space, and not into a space that is anywhere 'empty' but as force everywhere, as a play of forces and force-waves simultaneously one and 'many', accumulating here while diminishing there, an ocean of forces storming and flooding within themselves, eternally changing, eternally rushing back, with tremendous years of recurrence, with an ebb and a flood of its forms, shooting out from the simplest into the most multifarious, from the stillest, coldest, most rigid into the most fiery, wild, self-contradictory, and then coming home from abundance to simplicity, from the play of contradiction back to the pleasure of harmony, affirming itself even in this sameness of its courses and years, blessing itself as what must eternally return, as a becoming that knows no satiety, no surfeit, no fatigue – this, my *Dionysian* world of eternal self-creating, of eternal self-destroying, this mystery world of dual delights, this my beyond good and evil, without goal, unless there is a goal in the happiness of the circle, without will, unless a ring feels good will toward itself – do you want a *name* for this world? A *solution* to all its riddles? A *light* for you too, for you, the most secret, strongest, most intrepid, most midnightly? – *This world is the will to power – and nothing besides!* And you yourselves too are this will to power – and nothing besides![13]

13 NF 35[12], 1885; WLN, 38–9.

This fragment, certainly one of the most remarkable examples of Nietzschean prose, originally had a different ending, in which – instead of insisting upon the identity of eternal recurrence and will to power – Nietzsche characterized the circumscribed world of force, circumscribed within infinite time, almost tautologically as the world of eternal recurrence, as a 'ring of rings' to be accepted and blessed by those contemplating it.[14] This correction represents a decisive change, for it lets us connect the two philosophemes that dominate Nietzsche's philosophy from *Zarathustra* onward. Indeed, the new formulation is more precise than the crossed-out fragment quoted above in how it expresses what Nietzsche wanted to say without making metaphysical concessions to Schopenhauer.

Let us attempt to discover how Nietzsche arrived at the plan to write a work with the title *The Will to Power*. This occurred around August 1885. In a notebook of this period, we find the following title:

The Will to Power
Attempt
at a new interpretation
of everything that happens.[15]

To judge from the few examples cited above (to which many more could have been added), it would seem that this title encapsulates Nietzsche's meditations to date, while also indicating his work programme for the near future. 'Everything that happens' (within the cycle of eternal recurrence) can be *interpreted* as will to power. Here, Nietzsche turns from plastic

14 NF 35[68], 1885.
15 NF 39[1], 1885.

– we might say Dionysiac – expression to specific theoretical formulation. This is directly followed by a series of interrelated fragments in which Nietzsche both sketches out the contents of individual chapters of the work and randomly lists themes to be explored. Nutrition, reproduction, adaptation to the environment, heredity, division of labour are to be traced to the will to power, while pleasure and pain are to be analysed in relation to the will to power; the same goes for knowledge.[16] The body must form the common thread of these analyses; the will to truth, the will to justice, the will to beauty, the will to help others – all these are nothing other than will to power.[17] There follow a sort of Preface and Introduction.[18] In the Preface, Nietzsche proposes an interpretation of the world that does not depend on morality (for Nietzsche, to speak of natural laws means imposing moral representations on nature). Atheism, the negation of God, signifies an 'elevation of Man'; but, Nietzsche adds, if God – that is, the moral interpretation of the world – is refuted, the Devil – the popular expression for an immoral interpretation of reality – certainly is not. In the Introduction, however, Nietzsche lingers upon another idea, one that would become centrally important in subsequent sketches for a work on the will to power. He stresses that pessimism (which is ultimately a form of hedonism) is not the great danger, but rather the '*meaninglessness* of everything that happens! Moralistic interpretation has become invalid along with religious interpretation.' Modern thinkers have either not realized this, or they do not want to admit it, and although they may be atheists like Schopenhauer, they continue to attribute a

16 NF 39[12], 1885; NF 39[13], 1885.

17 NF 39[12], [13], 1885.

18 NF 39[14], [15], 1885.

moral significance to the world. However, morality and God are interdependent: if one falls, the other collapses. Nietzsche proposes to interpret the world in an 'immoral' way, such that 'our entire morality to date will appear as a special case' of a global interpretation (which would therefore be rather more 'extramoral' than 'immoral').[19]

This new 'interpretation of everything that happens' is expressed in the form of a reduction of our thinking, willing and feeling to value judgements, which correspond in turn to our instincts. These can in turn be reduced to the will to power, which is 'the final fact to which we can descend'.[20] In a fragmentary preface we read: 'Under the not innocuous title "The Will to Power" a new philosophy, or more precisely *the attempt at a new interpretation of everything that happens*, will hereby find expression: as is fitting, only provisionally and experimentally, only as preparation and by way of preliminary inquiry, only as a "prelude" to something serious that will require more initiated and elect ears, which is obvious when it comes to everything a philosopher says *publicly*.'[21]

In a subsequent fragment, Nietzsche stresses that, for him, there is no such thing as *Erscheinungen* (appearances, phenomena) as distinct from the essence of things; he would not have the 'will to power' be understood as a *noumenon*. For Nietzsche, appearance is the true and the only reality of things, not reality's opposite. He understands appearance as 'reality resisting transformation into an imaginative "truth-world"'. In its multiplicity and richness, appearance is inaccessible to 'logical procedures and distinctions'. Nietzsche suggests that 'will to power'

19 Ibid.

20 NF 40[61], 1885.

21 NF 40[50], 1885.

might be a particular name for this appearance-reality, 'defined from within and not based on its fluid, protean nature'.[22] Given this interpretation of reality, it is evident why Nietzsche goes on to speak, in following fragments, of the 'will to power' not only as a 'basic drive' (*Grundbegierde*),[23] to which – as expressed above – we can 'descend' as to a 'final fact', but also as a 'multiplicity of "wills to power"' in every person (and thus not as a single will to power distributed via the process of individuation). There we read: '*Man as a plurality of "wills to power": each with a multiplicity of means and forms of expression*. The individual *supposed* "passions" (e.g., man is "cruel") are merely fictitious unities: that which enters consciousness from the different fundamental drives as *of the same kind* becomes, through a synthesizing fiction, a "being" or "faculty" – a passion. Just as the "soul" itself is an *expression* of all the phenomena of consciousness which, however, we *interpret as the cause of all these phenomena* ("self-consciousness" is a fiction!).'[24]

We have dealt at some length with this first phase of the history of the will to power as a literary project and have tried to cast light on some (though not all) essential aspects of Nietzsche's thoughts on the subject because these aspects will recur in later plans, if with considerable modifications and shifts of emphasis, as well as changes in terminology. It bears mentioning that for a certain period of time, from late summer 1885 through spring 1886, the project of the 'Will to Power', which reappears in spring 1886 with the subtitle 'Attempt at a New Interpretation of the World', is not privileged over other titles and projects (which are more or

22 NF 40[53], 1885.

23 NF 1[58], 1885/86; WLN, 59.

24 NF 1[58], 1885/86; WLN, 60.

less interchangeable among themselves).[25] A decisive shift in Nietzsche's plans occurs only in the summer of 1886. In Sils-Maria, he writes down a new title (dated 'Sils-Maria, summer 1886'), or, more precisely, the old title with a new subtitle that he would retain until 26 August 1888. The new plan appears in a large notebook containing a great deal of material that Nietzsche transcribed for *Beyond Good and Evil* and other publications of that period.

The Will to Power.
Attempt
at a transvaluation of all values.
In four books.

First book: The danger of dangers (description of nihilism as the *necessary consequence of value judgements to date*).

Second book: Critique of values (of logic, etc.).

Third book: the problem of the legislator (here the history of solitude). *How* must those who subvert values be constituted? People who have *all* the qualities of the modern soul, but who are strong enough to transform them into health.

Fourth book: the hammer and the means to their task.

Sils-Maria, summer 1886[26]

25 NF 2[73], 1886.
26 NF 2[100], 1886.

This sketch puts the problem of values front and centre. The formula 'transvaluation of all values' (*Umwertung aller Werte*) remains the constant subtitle of all subsequent plans for *The Will to Power*. A year earlier, in June–July 1885, Nietzsche had already called it the principal task of free spirits to prepare a reversal or subversion of values (*Umkehrung der Werte*).[27] This requires the 'unleashing' of 'many instincts previously reined in and calumniated' against the ideals of the herd, against moral *tartufferie*, against the idealistic pessimism of the modern age.[28] Now Nietzsche places 'the danger of dangers' – that is, nihilism, understood as the inevitable consequence of the moral-Christian interpretation of life – at the beginning of his meditations. The imminent danger is that of meaninglessness, of the senselessness of all existence. Science, politics (nationalism and anarchism are named in the same breath), history all produce nihilistic consequences; and (with Wagner) art, too, leads to nihilism. Now Nietzsche's goal is no longer a new interpretation of everything that happens, but (here, we are nearly reminded of Marx's famous eleventh thesis on Feuerbach) the overthrow, subversion, transmutation, transvaluation, in short, the *Umwertung* of all values. The theme of nihilism and its overcoming thus becomes central in all Nietzsche's notes beginning in the summer of 1886. As for the literary project of *The Will to Power*, let us note that the four-part division is maintained in the overwhelming majority of plans for the project, and that these plans, appearing intermittently in the notebooks, mark the course of Nietzsche's meditations, serving as points of reference, of stocktaking and of new departures. The first book is dedicated to the description of nihilism, the second to the

27 NF 37[8], 1885; WLN, 32.

28 Ibid.

critique of values (or of morality), the third to the will to power as a determinant in the subversion of values. The content of the fourth book is not evident here, and it becomes less so in subsequent plans. Nietzsche speaks of the 'hammer' (a metaphor indicating the selectively destructive potential of the doctrine of eternal recurrence), of a terrible decision that must be provoked in Europe, which will slow the 'mediocritization' (*Vermittelmäßigung*) of Man, to which a decline, the end, would be preferable.[29]

Nietzsche announced *The Will to Power* on the back cover of *Beyond Good and Evil: Prelude to a Philosophy of the Future*, published in the summer of 1886. Only from this point onward can one legitimately speak of an intention on his part to publish a work in four parts with the title *The Will to Power: Attempt at a Transvaluation of All Values.*

3. Between the summer of 1886 and the summer of 1887, while still writing in his notebooks on the theme of the will to power, Nietzsche dedicated himself to republishing his writings, from *The Birth of Tragedy* through *The Gay Science* (the *Untimely Meditations* were not republished, while *Thus Spoke Zarathustra* was issued in a revised edition containing the first three parts; the fourth part remained a secret). The fragment on European nihilism, dated 'Lenzer Heide, 10 June 1887', constitutes a high point of Nietzsche's meditations.[30]

It is worth recalling here too the basic ideas of this fundamental text, which is generally known not in its authentic form, but from the mutilated version published in the so-called *Will to*

29 NF 2[131], 1885/86; WLN, 87.

30 NF 5[71], 1887; WLN, 116–21, from which the quotations in the following paragraph are taken [translation modified].

Power. 'The Christian moral hypothesis', Nietzsche writes, 'endowed man with an absolute *value*, in contrast to his smallness and contingency in the flux of becoming and passing away.' Recognizing sense even in the evil that is in the world, it affirmed the goodness of God and the perfection of the world. Finally, it presupposed in man an 'adequate knowledge' of absolute values. Thus morality 'shielded man from despising himself as man, from taking sides against life'; it was 'the great *antidote* to practical and theoretical *nihilism*'. But 'among the forces that morality cultivated was also "truthfulness": this, in the end, turns against morality, discovers its *teleology*, the *partiality* of its viewpoint'. Morality appears to truthfulness as mendacious, and at this point the desire to be liberated from the lies of morality acts as a stimulus against nihilism. Here, in fact, we find ourselves trapped in a contradiction: on the one hand, we do not appreciate the knowledge that we have attained (that is, the knowledge of the mendacity of the moral interpretation of the world); on the other hand, we are not permitted to appreciate the moral lies. This results in a process of dissolution. In Europe's contemporary situation, Nietzsche continues, the moderation of the value of man and of evil can be endured; the absurdity and the randomness of existence can still be tolerated. 'The power man has achieved now allows a *reduction* of those means of discipline of which the moral interpretation was the strongest. "God" is much too extreme a hypothesis.' But extreme hypotheses can be replaced only by other extreme hypotheses. Thus, the God hypothesis is succeeded by 'belief in the absolute immorality of nature', by diffidence toward any inquiry into the meaning of evil, or into there being any sense to existence in general. '*One* interpretation has perished; but because it was regarded as *the* interpretation, there now seems to be no meaning at all in existence, everything seems to be *in vain*.' The thought that everything is in vain is a paralysing thought that reaches its height in conjunction with the knowledge of the eternal recurrence of the same: 'nothingness ("meaninglessness") eternally!' But this is the 'European form of Buddhism'. In fact, eternal recurrence is 'the *most scientific* of all possible hypotheses'. If existence had a goal, in the course of infinite time it would already have been reached. Therefore, existence has no goal. The theory of eternal recurrence can be considered the opposite of pantheism, insofar as pantheism affirms the perfection, the eternity, the divinity of existence. Nietzsche asks, then, if the end of morality also entails the end of any affirmative position with regard to existence, that is, whether it is possible to 'say yes' to the process of the real after having distanced oneself from any teleological representation of it. 'This would be the case if something within that process were *achieved* at every moment of it – and always the same thing. Spinoza attained an affirmative stance like this insofar as every moment [within his pantheism] has a *logical* necessity', and 'in his basic instinct', Spinoza was logical. For Nietzsche, he is an exceptional case. In reality, '*every fundamental trait* which underlies everything that happens, which expresses itself in *everything* that happens, ought to lead an individual who felt it as *his* fundamental trait to welcome triumphantly every moment of general existence. The point would be precisely to experience this fundamental trait in oneself as good, as valuable, with pleasure.' Up until now, morality has rescued men from desperation and impotence because it taught the oppressed, taught people subject to violence, to hate and to scorn the basic character trait of those who have dominated through violence and oppression: that is, by means of the *will to power*. To negate, to undermine this morality means to take from the sufferers and the oppressors the right to scorn the will to power. This is precisely what one does by exposing the 'will to morality' as nothing other than a will to power: the hatred, the scorn for the will to power is itself a will to power. Thus, the oppressed find themselves on the same level as the oppressors, or, better: given that life itself is will to power, those who have 'come off badly' in life (*die Schlechtweggekommenen*) are no longer protected against nihilism. Once they have lost their faith in a morality hostile to the will to power, they are destined to perish, indeed destroying themselves in search of poisons, of drugs, of 'romanticism'; their will becomes a 'will to nothingness'. Nihilism is thus a symptom of the fact that those who have come off badly in life no longer have any moral consolation, any reason to live in a state of resignation, and this is why they desire their own end: the European form of Buddhism, attained once all existence has lost its 'meaning'. This does not mean that misery has generally increased in the modern age. The panacea 'God, morality, submission' was useful precisely when the misery was at its worst. Active nihilism, however, makes its appearance under relatively more favourable conditions. 'A certain intellectual fatigue, brought by the long struggle of philosophical opinions to the point of hopeless scepticism *toward* all philosophy, characterizes the position, by no means *lowly*, of these nihilists.' But what does it mean to have 'come off badly'? 'This phrase has above all a *physiological* significance, rather than a political one. The most unhealthy kind of man in Europe (in all social classes) is fertile ground for this nihilism: he will feel belief in eternal recurrence [that is, immanence without escape] to be a curse.' If one is struck by this curse, one no longer shies away from any sort of action, and abandons oneself to the pleasure of destruction. In Nietzsche's eyes, a crisis of this sort has the merit 'of *purifying*, of crowding related elements together . . . of assigning common tasks to men with opposite ways of thinking

– bringing to light the weaker, the more uncertain of them as well and thus initiating *an order of rank among forces*' within which it becomes evident who commands and who obeys. (Naturally – Nietzsche adds – 'outside all existing social orders'.) 'In this process, who will prove to be the strongest?' Nietzsche finally asks, answering: 'the most moderate, those who have no *need* of extreme articles of faith, those who not only concede but even love a good deal of contingency and nonsense, who can think of man with a considerable moderation of his value and not thereby become small and weak'; in sum, 'men who are *sure of their power* and who represent with conscious pride the strength man has achieved'. 'What would such a man think of eternal recurrence?' With this question Nietzsche ends this fragment, in which he tried to interconnect the fundamental themes of his philosophical reflections of 1887: nihilism, eternal recurrence, will to power.

Immediately thereafter, Nietzsche wrote *On the Genealogy of Morality*, in the course of a few weeks. In this 'polemic' he radically historicizes every type of morality. The commandments of morality are measured in relation to the social classes whose values they express. That is: that which is recognized as good was, in reality, good for the dominant classes, for those who were free, not for the oppressed. The concepts 'good' and 'evil' have a double origin: one with those who dominate, another with the oppressed. The master stroke of the oppressed was to have succeeded – through the agency of Christian priests – in imposing the morality of *ressentiment* upon the dominators, in infecting them with 'bad conscience'. Nietzsche contrasts the so-called morality of the masters with the 'morality of the slaves'. He understands Christian virtues as the virtues of the *canaille*. 'The social principles of Christianity preach cowardice, self-contempt, debasement, servility, humility, in short: all the qualities of the *canaille*', the young Marx had written forty years earlier, in 1847.[31]

After publishing the *Genealogy of Morality*, Nietzsche turned with concentrated force, between autumn 1887 and March 1888, to organizing and transcribing his notes for *The Will to Power*. The results of this intense labour are 372 numbered and indexed fragments in two quarto notebooks (W II 1 and W II 2) and on the first fifty-eight pages of a large folio notebook (W II 3). Another notebook (W II 4) contains the index. Next to summary descriptions of content Nietzsche also inscribed – for the first 300 numbers – a Roman numeral from I to IV, evidently referring to the four-part plan of *The Will to Power*. Nietzsche wrote to Peter Gast multiple times about his work: 'In the end, I do not want to conceal the fact that for me this entire time has been rich in synthetic insights and intuitions; that my courage has been renewed to do "the incredible" and to formulate unto its final consequences the philosophical sensibility that sets me apart from all others' (6 January 1888). 'Oh, how *instructive* it is to live in such an extreme state as mine! Now, for the first time, I understand *history*, I have never had deeper eyes than in these last months' (1 February 1888). And finally the most direct evidence of work on *The Will to Power*: 'I have completed the first draft of my "attempt at a transvaluation": all in all, it was torture, and I still don't have the courage for it. I shall try to do a better job of it ten years hence' (13 February 1888). 'You mustn't believe that I've made "literature" again: this draft was *for me*; every winter, one after another, I would like to write such a draft *for*

31 Karl Marx, 'Der Kommunismus des "Rheinischen Beobachters"', in Karl Marx and Friedrich Engels, *Werke*, vol. 4 (Berlin: Dietz Verlag, 1959), 200.

me – the thought of "publication" is really *out of the question*' (26 February 1888).

We find traces of what Nietzsche was reading during this period in the third of the notebooks containing the 'first draft' he speaks of: Baudelaire's *Posthumous Works* (just published in Paris, 1887), Tolstoy's *My Religion* (Paris, 1885), a work by the great Orientalist and biblical scholar Julius Wellhausen on Arab antiquity (*Remains of Arabic Paganism*, Berlin, 1887) as well as Wellhausen's *Prolegomena for the History of Israel* (Berlin, 1883), the first volume of the Goncourts' *Journal*, also recently published (Paris, 1887), *Some Reflections on German Theatre* by Benjamin Constant (1809), Renan's *Life of Jesus* (1863), and finally, and most importantly, Dostoevsky's *Demons* in French translation (*Les Possédés*, translated from the Russian by V. Derély, Paris, 1886). These readings are decisive, above all for the conception of primitive Christianity to which Nietzsche now dedicates a great deal of attention. Tolstoy's and Dostoevsky's books especially supply Nietzsche with key ideas for his polemic against Renan: Tolstoy with his psychology of the Redeemer, Dostoevsky with his history of the concept of God (which is related to the pan-Slavic theory of Dostoevsky's character Shatov). Nietzsche proved an excellent reader; what is more, these readings, like those of the preceding years (as the new historical-critical edition of his writings will carefully document), show a Nietzsche solidly anchored in the cultural problems of his time, a historical Nietzsche having little to do with the pale ghost of many interpretations – German ones above all – that have done little other than weave and reweave a dubious web of philosophemes without any concrete reference to Nietzsche's real intellectual life.

In the spring of 1888, first in Nice and then in Turin, Nietzsche keeps working at a fast clip. In the notebook chronologically following those described above (W II 5), original formulations outnumber excerpts from other authors, though there are plenty of transcriptions and reflections provoked by what he was reading, such as Victor Brochard's work *The Greek Sceptics* (Paris 1887), which gives Nietzsche an occasion to exalt the sceptical philosopher as the only philosopher possible today, or Charles Féré's *Degeneration and Criminality* (Paris 1888) on physiological degeneration and its social causes, an aspect of European decadence on which Nietzsche was currently focusing his attention. Finally, there is Louis Jacolliot's translation of the Indian legal code of Manu (*The Religious Legislators. Manu-Moses-Mohammed*, Paris 1876), which Nietzsche takes for the classic example of the religious *pia fraus* (pious fraud). Although up to this moment historical-psychological reflections on the pessimism–nihilism–Christianity nexus predominate, now the concept of *décadence* (in which all manifestations of pessimism, nihilism and Christianity converge) begins to come to the fore, along with a deepening of the epistemological-metaphysical aspect of the problem. Significantly, the latter is accompanied by a return to the antithesis 'art' and 'truth', from *The Birth of Tragedy*. In the notes for *The Birth of Tragedy* Nietzsche develops the problem of the 'true' and the 'apparent' world that we have already discussed with regard to the fragments of summer 1885. The conclusion these fragments lead up to can be found in the famous chapter of *Twilight of the Idols* titled 'How the "True World" Finally Became a Fable'. The belief in a 'true world' as over against an 'apparent' one conditions the complex of phenomena that Nietzsche successively uses the terms pessimism, nihilism and decadence to describe. And in fact the first chapter of the plan according to which Nietzsche indexed most of the notes in the notebook discussed above bears the title

'The True and the Apparent World'.[32] In this plan, Nietzsche makes clear the connection between the belief in a true world (be it philosophical, religious or moral) and decadence (that is, again: pessimism, nihilism, Christianity), also illuminating the contrary movements or 'countermovements' (Nietzsche speaks of *Gegenbewegungen*) against decadence. Thus, for example, the title he gives in the index to a series of fragments reflecting on *The Birth of Tragedy* is 'Countermovement: *art*!'[33] This attempt by Nietzsche to reorganize his own material is of interest when set in chronological sequence alongside his other plans of the period (as the new critical edition will do),[34] especially with regard to the literary architecture of the work he intended to write. This time the corresponding plan is not divided into four parts, but simply into chapters (eight to twelve of them, depending on the version):

1. Real and apparent world
2. Philosophers as a decadent type
3. Religion as an expression of decadence
4. Morality as an expression of decadence
5. The *countermovements*: why they have failed
6. Where does our modern world belong, to exhaustion or ascent? – its multiplicity and unrest are determined by the highest form of becoming conscious
7. The will to power: the *becoming-conscious* of the will to life . . .
8. The *therapeutics* of the future[35]

32 NF 14[169], 1888.

33 NF 14[14] ff., 1888.

34 [Or, rather, has done. Trans.]

35 NF 15[20], spring 1888.

In this version, the plan is projected to fill 600 pages, as we see from a calculation ('600 : 8') that Nietzsche wrote next to it. The theme of nihilism is replaced with that of decadence, at least in the title. Following further attempts at organizing his notes, which can be traced in the final volume of the posthumous fragments in the critical edition (1888–89), Nietzsche – having meanwhile written *The Case of Wagner*, a text dedicated to a typical example of modern decadence – undertakes to transcribe a fair copy of the notes collected in the notebooks from autumn 1887 to spring 1888. The transcription, begun in Turin near the end of spring, is continued in Sils-Maria in the summer of 1888. Toward the middle of August Nietzsche begins to transcribe and rework his notes, regrouping them according to his themes. The last Sunday in August – that is, the 26th – is the date Nietzsche inscribed on the final plan for a work to be titled *The Will to Power: Attempt at a Transvaluation of All Values*. Shortly thereafter, he modifies his literary intentions, which is why it is worth reproducing this final plan in full:

Sketch of
the plan for:
The Will to Power
Attempt
at a transvaluation of all values
– *Sils-Maria*
last Sunday in
the month of August 1888

We Hyperboreans. – *Laying the foundations for the problem.*

Book One: *'What is truth?'*

Chapter One: Psychology of error.
Chapter Two: Value of truth and error.
Chapter Three: The will to power (justified solely by its positive value for life).

Book Two: *Origin of values.*

Chapter One: The metaphysicians.
Chapter Two: The *homines religiosi.*
Chapter Three: Good people and those who would make things better.

Book Three: *Conflict of values.*

Chapter One: Thoughts on Christianity.
Chapter Two: On the physiology of art.
Chapter Three: On the history of European nihilism.

A psychologist's pastime.

Book Four: *The great midday.*

Chapter One: The principle of life: 'hierarchy'.
Chapter Two: The two paths.
Chapter Three: Eternal recurrence.[36]

In this plan, the problem of 'values' is dominant (the value of truth and error, the value of the will to power, the origin of values,

36 NF 18[17], 1888.

the conflict of values), and Nietzsche returns to the 'history of European nihilism'. But he scraps this plan as well shortly thereafter, after using it to index fragments stretching back to 1883. The decisive change in Nietzsche's plans occurs between the last days of August and the first days of September, when he sketches out a new plan under the title *Transvaluation of All Values* (the main title, *Will to Power*, has disappeared in this draft), based on the material that he had already *effectively* elaborated. The new plan consisted of twelve chapters:

1. *We Hyperboreans.*
2. *The problem of Socrates.*
3. *Reason in philosophy.*
4. *How the true world finally became a fable.*
5. *Morality as anti-nature.*
6. *The four great errors.*
7. *For us – against us.*
8. *Concept of a religion of decadence.*
9. *Buddhism and Christianity.*
10. *From my aesthetics.*
11. *Among artists and writers.*
12. *Maxims and arrows.*[37]

A manuscript in twelve chapters really existed at this point and can indeed be reconstructed today through a careful examination of the definitive manuscripts of the works that Nietzsche shortly thereafter decided to publish, abandoning the plan of *The Will to Power*: the manuscripts of *Twilight of the Idols* and *The Antichrist*. Numbers 2, 3, 4, 5, 6 and 12 in the plan become chapters bearing precisely the same titles in *Twilight of the Idols*, and 10 and 11 are

37 NF 19[4], 1888.

combined in the chapter of that work bearing the title 'Skirmishes of an Untimely Man'. Numbers 1, 7, 8 and 9 correspond to the original titles, later crossed out by Nietzsche, of the first four groups of paragraphs in *The Antichrist*: 'We Hyperboreans', paragraphs 1–7; 'For us – against us', paragraphs 8–14; 'Concept of a religion of decadence', paragraphs 15–19; 'Buddhism and Christianity', paragraphs 20–30. The sections cited from *Twilight of the Idols* and the first twenty-three paragraphs of *The Antichrist* thus belong originally to the same manuscript, which Nietzsche regarded for a time as the *Transvaluation of All Values*. At this point, Nietzsche once again decided to modify his programme with regard to the plan of 26 August 1888 (which is similar in many respects to the twelve-chapter plan), extracting chapters 1, 7, 8 and 9 from the manuscript to use them in a work about Christianity (already bearing the title 'We Hyperboreans', which was also the Introduction in the plan of 26 August 1888), and with what was left he composed a 'compendium' of his philosophy (initially titled *Idleness of a Psychologist*, then *Twilight of the Idols*). Thus was the new work programme established: Nietzsche's future *magnum opus* was to be titled *Transvaluation of All Values* and would be published in four books, the first of which would bear the title *The Antichrist* (twenty-three chapters of this work were already written by the beginning of September, as we have seen). After this point we find various plans in Nietzsche's manuscripts under the collective title *Transvaluation of All Values*, and no longer under the title *The Will to Power*. For example:

Transvaluation of All Values

Book One.

The Antichrist. Attempt at a critique of Christianity.

Book Two.

The free spirit. Critique of philosophy as a nihilistic movement.

Book Three.

The immoralist. Critique of the most fateful kind of ignorance: morality.

Book Four.

Dionysus. Philosophy of eternal recurrence.[38]

The content of the new work does not depart substantially from the themes we have seen developed in the plans for *The Will to Power*. This demonstrates that, for Nietzsche, the literary plan of the *Transvaluation* in four books was destined to replace the plan of *The Will to Power*, and, in fact, the material of *The Antichrist* is drawn from notes composed in the preceding months, when he was thinking about *The Will to Power*. What in these notes he could not use in the new project was collected in *The Twilight of the Idols*, which Nietzsche described in a letter to Peter Gast as 'a daringly and precisely thrown-together summary' of his 'essential philosophical *heterodoxies*' (12 September 1888).

On 21 September 1888, Nietzsche was once again in Turin. In nine days, he managed to finish the first book of the *Transvaluation of All Values*, that is *The Antichrist*. The date 30 September 1888 acquires symbolic significance for Nietzsche: he inserts it below the Preface to *Twilight of the Idols*, and at the end of *The Antichrist* we read: 'We calculate time from this *dies nefastus* with which this fatality began – from the *first* day of

38 NF 19[8], 1888.

Christianity! – *Why not, preferably, from its last? – From today?* – Transvaluation of all values!'

A state of exaltation takes hold of Nietzsche. After this he no longer knows any limits. To *The Antichrist* he adds a 'law against Christianity', introduced as follows: '*Given on the day of salvation, on the first day of Year One (– on 30 September 1888 by the false chronology).*' Reading Nietzsche's statements about his work, one hardly registers the historical-critical significance of *The Antichrist*, which (as Franz Overbeck would later note) includes some real *tours de force*, like the psychology of the Redeemer and that of the apostle Paul, the historical reconstruction of the origins of the Christian movement, and the analysis of the religious *pia fraus*. *Ecce Homo* arises from this state of euphoria, beginning in mid-October 1888 as a development of a chapter that Nietzsche had added to *Twilight of the Idols*. Nietzsche's notebooks also contain some notes for another book of the *Transvaluation*: 'The Immoralist'. But this project is interrupted by *Ecce Homo*, until Nietzsche writes in a letter of 20 November to Georg Brandes that he has finished the entire *Transvaluation*, by which he means *The Antichrist*. To Paul Deussen as well Nietzsche writes on 26 November 1888: 'My life is now reaching its apex: a few more years, and the earth will be shaken by an enormous thunderbolt. – I swear to you that I have the force *to change how the years are counted*. – Nothing that stands today will remain standing, I am more dynamite than man. – My transvaluation of all values, with the main title *The Antichrist*, is finished.' And, in fact, on the final title page, we read: *The Antichrist. Transvaluation of All Values*. The collective title of a work in four books has now become the subtitle of *The Antichrist*. In the end, Nietzsche will cross out the subtitle *Transvaluation of All Values* and replace it with another: *A Curse on Christianity*. From his exalted perspective, Nietzsche's last writings are no longer literary events, 'but a shattering of all that exists'.[39] Thus ends the literary project of *The Will to Power*, at the very threshold of Nietzsche's own end.

4. After all we have said, it should be clear that the only way to get to know all the possibilities or 'impossibilities' implied by the mass of notes left by Nietzsche in the last years of his conscious life is not to organize this material according to one or another of his plans (not even the last in the series), but, rather, to publish everything just as it appears in the manuscripts and in strict chronological order, omitting only the fragments that Nietzsche used in his published works. This is the objection first raised by August Horneffer (1906) and then by Richard Roos (1956) and Karl Schlechta (1956) against the collection of fragments that Peter Gast and Elisabeth Förster-Nietzsche published under the title *The Will to Power* and declared Nietzsche's *magnum opus*, purportedly realized according to the intentions of the author.

We have dwelt upon all these details so as to try to give an approximate idea of the difficulty inherent in any attempt to extract Nietzsche's 'philosophy of the future' from the mass of his posthumous notes, which reveal a great deal of uncertainty and show, in the final analysis, that Nietzsche did *not* achieve his 'transvaluation of all values'. Their significance lies entirely in the possibility they offer of reconstructing Nietzsche's attempt as such. The study of the unpublished material that this task requires, as well as the reconstruction of the data from which Nietzsche started, of what he knew and of what he read, is just beginning. To us, it would seem that the principal and decisive reason for the failure of his ambitious philosophical project is that, for Nietzsche, philosophy can no longer justify its existence as a theoretical activity: history, as he himself

39 Letter to C. G. Naumann, 26 November 1888.

said, has replaced it. Philosophy's successor would have had to be a legislator, and Nietzsche's ambition, the purview of his 'transvaluation of all values', is to give humanity a new law. Philosophy as history is the *pars destruens* of Nietzsche's late thinking (analyses of European nihilism, destruction of the metaphysical formula 'the true world', anti-Christianity). In the transition to the constructive part of his philosophy, Nietzsche finds himself caught in an irreconcilable contradiction between his own extreme scepticism, his struggle against any convictions, and the need to 'legislate'. Nietzsche reserved the fourth book for his legislation in nearly every plan for *The Will to Power* and then for the *Transvaluation of All Values*. According to the final plan cited above, this was to follow the critique of Christianity ('The Antichrist'), of philosophy ('The Free Spirit') and of morality ('The Immoralist'), and would bear the title 'Dionysus: Philosophy of Eternal Recurrence'. As a radical negation of any consolatory transcendence, the theory of the eternal recurrence of the same has, in fact, a selective function: only those who can bear it have what it takes to become the new man, the individual Nietzsche desires. Nonetheless, not a single fragment exists that could shed light on this peculiar utopia. Certainly, Nietzsche detested his present, from German nationalism to antisemitism, socialism and anarchism, but he did not leave a single line suggesting an alternative to the political, social, moral and cultural phenomena he criticized. Nietzsche is a destroyer, not a creator, of myths. *Naufragium feci, bene navigavi* [I wrecked the ship, I sailed well], the epigraph set atop one of the prefaces written during the spring and summer of 1888, emblematically indicates the outcome of his philosophy.[40] The 'shipwreck' is an integral part

40 NF 16[44], 1888. [The saying is attributed to the Greek Stoic philosopher Zeno; cf. Diogenes Laertius, *Lives of Eminent Philosophers, 7. 1 Zeno*, trans. R. D. Hicks (Cambridge, MA: Harvard University Press, 1931), vol. 2, 115. Trans.].

of the programme. This proves yet again – if such proof were needed – how arbitrary it was to create a systematic philosophy by cobbling together fragments scattered across multiple notebooks and selling it to the European public under the title The *Will to Power* in the first years of the twentieth century. The posthumous papers, which could have helped relativize and de-dogmatize Nietzsche's positions, were used with precisely the opposite intention: to provide a system to interpreters avid to add one to the extant series of philosophical systems. The suspense of 'thought in the making' did not interest the simplifiers, from Peter Gast to Alfred Bäumler.

The thoroughly disparate judgements passed on Nietzsche by his two closest friends, Erwin Rohde and Franz Overbeck, nicely illustrate the contrary uses that his thought can be put to generally. After reading *Beyond Good and Evil*, Erwin Rohde wrote to Overbeck:

> I read most of it with great vexation. For the most part, it consists of discourses by someone who has eaten too much, occasionally elevated by the stimulating effect of wine, but filled with a repugnant disgust for everything and everyone. What there is in it of philosophy is as meagre and as nearly childish as the political content is silly and ignorant of the world. Still, there are some witty *aperçus* in there, as well as some captivating dithyrambic passages. But it's still all arbitrary inspirations; there are no more convictions to be found there; a particular point of view is taken *capriciously* and everything is made to flow therefrom, as if this were the only point of view existing in the world. And then the next time, of course, the contrary point of view is taken and praised just as unilaterally. *I* am no longer able to take these eternal metamorphoses seriously. They are a hermit's visions

and ideational soap bubbles which doubtless afford pleasure and distraction to the hermit, but why communicate that to the *world* as a sort of gospel? And then this constant annunciation of tremendous things, hair-raising audacities of thought, that – to the reader's bored disappointment – *never come*! – I find this inexpressibly repulsive . . . To me it seems perfectly justified that this sort of thing has no effect; really, nothing will come of it; it all just runs through one's fingers like sand. Finally, what substantive ideas is one really left with in the end? A flickering and flaring before one's eyes, no beautiful steady illuminating light emanates from this book. What it says about the *herd* character of humanity today is good, but how is one supposed to conceive of what Nietzsche fantastically imagines as a cannibalistic morality, dictatorially imposed? *What* sign of the times points to this grandiloquent berserker of the future? (Whose picture it seems to me he's painted on the wall for us so often that he himself has had enough of it.) – In short, to be honest, the book really annoyed me very much, and more than anything the author's *gigantic* vanity, which is apparent less in the way he secretly and openly takes *himself*, with all his most personal traits, as a model for the coming Messiah, than in the fact that he is no longer able to comprehend *any* other tendency, even any occupation other than the one *he* is pleased to recognize at a given moment, as human or as valuable in any way. This is outrageous, given the *sterility* peering out from all corners of this essentially derivative mind. This might be explicable in the case of a *positive* spirit, however one-sided: but in the end Nietzsche is and remains a critic, and he should be able to sense that the one-sided nature of *productivity* suits him like a lion's pelt does an ass. – This book causes me more pain on our account than on

> his: he hasn't found the path that could lead him to self-fulfilment, and he's convulsively whipping himself back and forth, while demanding that this be taken for *evolution*. For our part, we may not be content with ourselves, but we don't demand any special veneration for our inadequacy. He would have to *work* honestly and in a workmanlike way for once to realize the value of flitting about like this between all manner of things, of stuffing oneself with impressions and insights: no value at all! . . . Do you know what I fear and envision occurring in Nietzsche's later years? That he will crawl to the *Cross*, from disgust with everything and because of the veneration for anything *distinguished* that has always been in his blood but which has now found a really unpleasant theoretical glorification.[41]

Overbeck replies:

> Although I will concede at least half of what you reproach the book and the person of its author with, still I believe you are speaking in anger. I myself can share this anger only very partially, and not in the least where you are most violently incensed. The political parts, for instance, don't bother me much, even if in his latest book Nietzsche 'politicizes' far too much for my tastes. Not because it exposes him overmuch to reproach for being 'ignorant about the world', for this objection doesn't seem very decisive to me, but because really politics 'doesn't matter to him' and cannot be dealt with *coram publico* in this way, while the tone is unpleasantly unlike what one might wish for in such a book . . . Also, the book

41 1 September 1886, in Patzer, ed., *Franz Overbeck–Erwin Rohde. Briefwechsel*, 108–9.

failed entirely to *further* enlighten me, at least, with regard to the aims of the author, his ultimate insights and intentions; after *Zarathustra* it seems a true retrogression, which is particularly worrisome in hermits' books of this kind. Also, I feel that some things in the book are excessively offensive . . . As you can see, I have no intention of being an apologist for anything, especially not for this book, yet there's nothing in today's literature that I find myself reading with such intellectual pleasure . . . Despite what to judge from this book seems an increasing dilettantism, Nietzsche's books guide the scholar, or anyway the scholar in me, more intimately into the heart of things than the monuments of a more methodical way of proceeding that are normally erected these days. As far as the author himself is concerned: You speak of gigantic vanity. I feel unable to contradict you entirely, but still this vanity is of a very particular kind. It seems to me that even in this book, and even for the reader who is otherwise unacquainted with its author, this vanity is mixed with another, completely different sentiment. Generally speaking, I don't know anyone besides Nietzsche who makes life so difficult for himself in order to be in accord with himself. In an era so tending to herd behaviour, the fact that this is expressed in such a monstrous way is not necessarily a personal fault. And this is how I would respond to most of your objections: in the abstract and initially I agree, but on the whole and in the end I am of a different opinion.[42]

Rohde's reaction to reading a book like *Beyond Good and Evil* might seem unjust and peevish, but it makes sense if one takes

42 23 September 1886, in Patzer, ed., *Franz Overbeck–Erwin Rohde. Briefwechsel*, 111–12.

Nietzsche at his word and understands his posing literally, as Rohde does here, and if one allows oneself to be impressed by his prophetic stance and his continual promises of things never yet seen. Of course, in this case, it is possible to have an equal but opposite, positive, reaction, that of the Nietzsche devotee: at least at the turn of the century, Nietzsche was truly a sort of Messiah for many weak-minded European intellectuals. The serene judgement of an independent spirit like Franz Overbeck is however the most appropriate one. And it was also precisely Overbeck who left the most important personal testimony of all those who knew Nietzsche intimately. He wrote: 'Nietzsche is the person in whose company I breathed in the freest possible way.'[43] Whoever does not feel himself breathing more freely after reading Nietzsche should stay far away from him, so as not to become a caricature, so as not to end up a Nietzschean. Reading Nietzsche's posthumous fragments in their original form without insisting on finding a system in them has a relativizing effect that should facilitate a free engagement with his thought.

5. Beginning in the spring of 1888 – that is, from his first days in Turin – everything Nietzsche writes, including his letters, is marked by an unspeakable psychic tension, which also manifests as euphoria. The illness has begun its work of devastation, and it is only with regard to these final manifestations that we can speak of Nietzsche's illness influencing his thought, although it is a nearly impossible task concretely to show where and when the dementia begins as long as Nietzsche is in command of his expressive abilities. *The Case of Wagner*, *Twilight of the Idols*, *The Antichrist*, *Ecce Homo*, *Nietzsche contra Wagner* and the

43 Carl Albrecht Bernoulli, *Franz Overbeck und Friedrich Nietzsche. Eine Freundschaft*, vol. 2 (Jena: Diederichs, 1908), 423.

Dithyrambs of Dionysus were all written between May of 1888 and 2 January 1889.

Ecce Homo contains some of Nietzsche's most beautiful pages, and not only that: many key aspects of his personality first come to light in these pages. But *Ecce Homo* cannot be considered a 'finished' text either, because Nietzsche continues to work on it up to the final day of his conscious life, adding parts and changing things even after his revision of the manuscript at the beginning of December. This is why it is particularly important, while reading, to be aware of the order in which Nietzsche composed the various paragraphs. It is certainly not a matter of indifference to know what was written during the composition of *Twilight of the Idols* and what precedes the collapse into psychic darkness by a matter of days.

Nietzsche spends the first two days in January preparing the manuscript of the *Dithyrambs of Dionysus*. On 3 January, he collapses, senseless, in the piazza Carlo Alberto in Turin. Between the 3rd and the 8th of January, he sends the so-called insanity notes to all his friends, to princes and statesmen, including Bismarck and the Italian king Umberto I (many of these notes were not mailed), signing them with 'Dionysus', 'Nietzsche-Caesar', 'Dionysus-the Crucified'. Cosima Wagner, too, receives three of these notes, in which she has become his wife (Nietzsche calls her Arianna, or Cosima-Arianna) and is told that she must announce the 'good news' to all mankind on Dionysus-Nietzsche's behalf. In his political proclamations, Nietzsche declares that he intends to 'have all the antisemites shot', and that he is working to form a European 'anti-German league' with the goal of provoking Germany to a 'war of desperation'.[44] 'My dear Professor,' he

44 Letter to Franz Overbeck, 4 January 1889; Letter to Franz Overbeck, 26 December 1888.

writes to Jacob Burckhardt on 6 January, 'in the end I would much rather be a Basel professor than God; but I have not dared to push my personal egotism so far as to have neglected on that account to create the world.'

On 9 January, Overbeck brings his friend, now insane, back from Turin.

5
Nietzsche and the 'Consequences'

1. In the final months of his conscious life, Nietzsche had some presentiment of his coming fame. It is worth keeping in mind that he undertook a lucid and coherent attempt to reinterpret his entire past – both his life and, especially, his works, from *The Birth of Tragedy* onward. This is why it is no exaggeration to speak of the compositions of 1888 – *The Case of Wagner*, *Twilight of the Idols*, *Nietzsche contra Wagner* and above all *Ecce Homo* – as 'propaganda writings'.[1] This self-reinterpretation should not be taken literally, neither with regard to Nietzsche's biography nor with regard to his thought. *Ecce Homo* is more like a new disguise, a new masquerade: 'I have a terrible fear that one day I will be pronounced *holy*,' he writes in the last chapter. 'You will guess why I am publishing this book *beforehand*; it shall prevent people from doing mischief with me. I do not want to be a holy man; sooner even a buffoon. – Perhaps I am a buffoon. – Yet in spite of that – or rather *not* in spite of it, because so far nobody has been more mendacious than holy men – the truth speaks out of me.'[2] But this 'demystifying' masquerade has had no effect whatsoever

1 Richard Roos, 'Les derniers écrits de Nietzsche et leur publication', *Revue philosophique de la France et de l'étranger* 2 (1956): 262–87 (here, 270).

2 *Ecce Homo*, 'Why I Am a Destiny', 1, in *On the Genealogy of Morals* and *Ecce Homo*, translated with commentary by Walter Kaufmann (New York: Vintage, 1969), 326 [translation modified].

in the shaping of Nietzsche's fame. When *Ecce Homo* was first published in 1908 as an independent work, in a deluxe edition with a cover designed by Henry van de Velde, Nietzsche had already been canonized. Elisabeth Förster-Nietzsche had already made use, in her way, of parts of this text to consolidate her own pretentions to being the sole trustworthy witness to her brother's life and to add some flavour here and there to the thin, insipid broth of her biography. Yet precisely the 1,300 large octavo pages in which she told the story of Nietzsche's life were crucial to the canonization process. One can no longer read these pages – dominated as they are by ignorant pretentiousness and the sickly-sweet idealism of the 'Naumburg virtue' that Nietzsche disliked in his sister,[3] but never by what he called the 'will to truth' – without oscillating between stupor and nausea. This book was the main source of the image of Nietzsche that nearly everyone engaging with him had to deal with practically up to the end of the Second World War, an image that formed the so-called Nietzscheans as it formed the equally so-called anti-Nietzscheans. Familial piety does not fully explain the apologetic and edifying tone of these pages. It is equally misleading to speak of conscious falsification, for what is shocking about the book is not the adjustment of facts to a preconceived schema, but Förster-Nietzsche's absolute 'good faith'. One is occasionally tempted to laugh, such as when we are surprised by a comparison between Nietzsche's and Goethe's personal appearances (Goethe is supposed to have had shorter legs than Nietzsche). No: It remains an important task of the scholarship on Nietzsche and his 'consequences' to establish with care the degree to which the sister's hagiography informed such writers as Charles Andler and Thomas Mann (a great deal, in our opinion). Nobody could imagine that the real Elisabeth Nietzsche

3 Letter to Franz Overbeck, 9 September 1882.

had already declared *her* true opinion of her brother in September 1882, when she saw her 'ideal' crumble in the face of Nietzsche's encounter with Lou Salomé: 'Do not read my brother's books,' she wrote to a friend in a twenty-page letter full of the kind of ridiculous gossip that helped bring her brother to the brink of suicide during the winter of 1882–83, 'they are too horrible for us, our hearts have higher aspirations than the exclusive exaltation of egotism. Ah! And do not try to bring these books into harmony with the Nietzsche of before, it is impossible, for Oh! my dear Clara, tell this to nobody, but I have had a terrible time here [in Tautenburg, where Lou was Nietzsche's guest]. I must admit that Fritz has changed, he *is* so much like his books.'[4] If there is anything Nietzsche truly suffered from, it is this 'Naumburg virtue', the hypocritical and self-assured moralism of the milieu he had grown up in. As late as in notes of autumn 1888 for *The Immoralist*, Nietzsche aims his critique at a purely petit-bourgeois morality with obvious origins in the 'pastor's house'. And, when Zarathustra says 'Good people never speak the truth' or 'Everything has been made duplicitous and twisted from the ground up by the good', when he speaks of 'the good and the righteous', these words can easily be replaced with 'my mother and my sister and all the innumerable Christians who are like them'.[5] Further, the so-called man of the herd is none other than the man of the 'middle classes' – as a fragment of 1888 explicitly states.[6]

---

4 24 September–2 October 1882 to Clara Geltzer, in Ernst Pfeiffer, ed., *Friedrich Nietzsche, Paul Rée, Lou von Salomé. Die Dokumente ihrer Begegnung* (Frankfurt am Main: Insel, 1970), 251–2.

5 *Thus Spoke Zarathustra*, Third Part, 'On Old and New Tablets', 7 and 28, 160 and 172 [translation modified.]

6 NF 15[47], 1888.

All this might somewhat diminish the titanic quality of Nietzsche's 'campaign against morality', of his 'immoralism', but it is, nonetheless, an integral part of it. H. Landry has observed that 'it is hard to find a period in history that was more hypocritical than the one Nietzsche lived in', especially – we would add – if one considers the social milieu in which he was educated.[7]

Between 1890 and 1894, the 'small, scattered readership that Nietzsche had always had' and who attentively followed his publications became 'a great horde of followers . . . Individual ideas of his, taken out of context and thus interpretable at will, became catchwords and slogans for entire trends, echoing in the conflict of opinions, in disputes between parties that were always entirely foreign to him.'[8] Thus did Lou von Salomé describe the initial 'consequences' of Nietzsche's work in the book she wrote about him in 1894 and which is still today one of the best that has ever been written about him because it arose from a brief but extremely intense exchange of ideas between the young Lou and Nietzsche himself. At least half the book is derived from direct testimonies that Lou was able to collect during those months in 1882. These 'consequences' were already in full gear when Förster-Nietzsche, definitively back from Paraguay, founded the Nietzsche-Archive and began her work of 'canonization'. Whereas the colonial project of the antisemitic husband (whom Nietzsche detested, as we have already noted) had failed, the new editorial project promised great success. Elisabeth Förster-Nietzsche thus stopped the complete edition of Nietzsche's works that Gast had begun to publish (admittedly with 'improvements' on Nietzsche's style!), and concentrated in her own hands everything that could be put to use in publishing her brother's works and letters. Even though, starting with Georg Brandes's Copenhagen lectures

7 Harald Landry, *Friedrich Nietzsche* (Berlin: Wegweiser, 1931), 223–4.

8 Andreas-Salomé, *Friedrich Nietzsche in seinen Werken*, 32.

of spring 1888, Nietzsche's fame and his influence on the various literary and philosophical currents of his time had already won some autonomy from the archive, now the latter became a sort of 'Mecca' for Nietzscheans of all stripes. Nietzsche's works enjoyed sensational print runs; for the remaining years of his life, privileged visitors were admitted to the presence of the poor human wreck of the man. Later, portraits and statuettes and a prettified version of the death mask were sold to the Nietzsche devotees.

The reaction to this cult was not long in coming. Its most serious and most engaged versions emanated from Basel, where there were still living memories of Nietzsche, thanks, above all, to the presence of Franz Overbeck. The conflict between the Nietzsche-Archive in Weimar and the Basel group of Nietzsche admirers (Carl Joël and Carl Albrecht Bernoulli, in particular) constitutes an extremely unpleasant and hardly edifying chapter in the story of Nietzsche's 'fortunes' (it might be better to speak of 'misfortunes'). Suffice it to say that Overbeck, who was already gravely ill, had the last days of his life poisoned by the calumnies of Förster-Nietzsche as well as those of Peter Gast (who had reconciled with Nietzsche's sister in 1899 and had offered her indispensable help in deciphering the notebooks preserved in the archive). Overbeck was accused of having failed to collect the letters of his demented friend and of having entered Nietzsche's syphilitic infection into the log of the clinic at Jena. These were baseless accusations, but they were propagated extremely unscrupulously by the archive in Weimar at the instigation of Nietzsche's sister and, for a time, with the support of Gast. Nietzsche's illness suddenly became a field of contention for the various factions. The well-known psychopathologist Paul Julius Möbius wrote an essay on the pathological elements in Nietzsche's work. There were investigations and counter-investigations of the family's hereditary taint, and hypotheses regarding the nature of

Nietzsche's paralysis were advanced by both sides to support their assessments of his philosophy's value. The *querelle allemande* of which Blunck has spoken assumed comic proportions. But the reaction against the hagiographic distortions of Nietzsche's sister wound up being influenced by the very positions it was revolting against. Every biographical problem was approached within the parameters set by Förster-Nietzsche's biography and her countless further publications. Thus, for example, it became obligatory to decide whether Wagner had betrayed Nietzsche, or vice versa; whether Paul Rée had tricked him in the episode with Lou or if Nietzsche had proven his moral turpitude in behaving as he did with his two friends; whether Overbeck believed in Nietzsche's 'greatness' or not; whether Nietzsche had been misunderstood as a friend or had betrayed all his friends; whether Nietzsche had been a saint, or sexually deficient, or a frequenter of prostitutes; whether or not Nietzsche had known Max Stirner's *The Ego and Its Own* (which, for unfathomable reasons, Förster-Nietzsche found a particularly reprehensible idea); whether he had taken his ideas from this or that author, or whether all his ideas were original.

Yet these controversies make up only a small part of the story of Nietzsche's fame. The followers and the enemies of his philosophy, unfazed by the critical or biographical scholarship, took what they wanted from the motley arsenal of Nietzsche's writings to support their own points of view. This is especially true of the literati, artists, poets and novelists, dramatists and philosophical dilettantes. Often enough it was not ideas they selected to serve their needs, but simply formulae, adapted in more or less bizarre ways. An ape with a lion's mask graces the cover of a book of 1897 by Leo Berg on the *Übermensch* in modern literature. The era produced countless friends of the *Übermensch*, but they were all more or less apes wearing lion masks. *Thus Spoke Zarathustra* was the book most often read. Gabriele D'Annunzio and Knut Hamsun, Hermann Sudermann and Frank Wedekind, Richard Dehmel and Gerhart Hauptmann all believed that they knew what the *Übermensch* was. Obviously, it is not our task here to reconstruct the history of Nietzsche's influence on European literature from the turn of the last century to the present day; suffice it to say that – as is usual in such cases – we have here to do with a quantity of more or less productive misunderstandings of Nietzsche whose value depends on the intrinsic quality of the works they inspired. To name only the most significant names: Thomas Mann and Robert Musil, Heinrich Mann and Stefan George, and then Rainer Maria Rilke and Hugo von Hofmannsthal, Stefan Zweig and Gottfried Benn – all were more or less influenced by Nietzsche. There is no complete study of this subject as yet, although there have been some recent initial attempts to critically reexamine Nietzsche's effect on modern literature, as well as numerous partial studies. Outside of Germany, Nietzsche has been especially popular in France (André Gide, Paul Valéry and Romain Rolland, but also André Malraux and Albert Camus, Jean-Paul Sartre and Gabriel Marcel, to name just a few). The simplified Nietzsche of the *Übermensch* and the 'will to power' (reduced to simple phrases) is central here too. Meanwhile, the Nietzsche legend has flourished, supported and fuelled by the 'studies' of various devotees building on the work of Elisabeth Förster-Nietzsche and her archive. Following Richard M. Meyer's insertion of Nietzsche into the 'system' of Wilhelmine Germany (1913), there appeared the great mythological imposture of Ernst Bertram (a disciple of Stefan George), who composed his book *Nietzsche: Attempt at a Mythology* (1918) for the initiated.[9] Everything became a 'myth' in this well-written, ostensibly profound book: by then,

9 Richard M. Meyer, *Nietzsche. Sein Leben und seine Werke* (Munich: Beck, 1913). Ernst Bertram, *Nietzsche. Versuch einer Mythologie* (Berlin: Bondi, 1918).

Wilhelmine Germany had collapsed, and so people found refuge from the difficult, nihilistic reality of the first postwar years in 'Eleusinian' mysteries and in the 'mythical' value of every event, and thus also of Nietzsche's life. This was however the high road to Nietzsche's appropriation by the Third Reich (Bertram would also become a National Socialist). The defeated German petite bourgeoisie, gradually regaining its strength, hardly knew what to do with Bertram's (and to some degree Thomas Mann's) 'mystified' Nietzsche. Yet precisely this Nietzsche (like the related versions of Ludwig Klages and Kurt Hildebrandt) could hardly resist the new mythology of blood and soil: the 'destruction of reason' in Nietzsche's work is triumphantly carried to term by Alfred Bäumler, the official writer of prefaces to Nietzsche's works in the 1930s. Nietzsche becomes Nordic and '*ur*-Germanic'. Naturally, there was no shortage of contrary voices raised against a still rather disquieting philosophy that was too intellectual and cultured to really serve the barbaric aims of Goebbels's 'mass hysteria'. These were however not the voices of the more serious adversaries of National Socialism – that is, of the Marxists, such as for example György Lukács, who considered Bäumler's and Alfred Rosenberg's usurpation of Nietzsche's philosophy fully legitimate. The most eloquent voice emerged from the ranks of the National Socialists themselves. The Wagnerian writer Curt von Westernhagen twice managed to marshal all his anti-Nietzschean passion in order to demonstrate that the true prophet of the 'heroic sage' Adolf Hitler was not the author of *Thus Spoke Zarathustra*, but Richard Wagner. Nietzsche's anti-Germanism and anti-antisemitism are just as easily demonstrable as Wagner's Teutonicism and rabid hatred of the Jews. No one listened to Westernhagen, and his two books full of Wagnerian Germanism and praise for the National Socialist Führer – *Wagner's Struggle Against Alien Spiritual Domination* (1935) and *Nietzsche, Jews, Anti-Jews* (1936) – were confiscated by the Nazis. Authoritative representatives of German culture (like Martin Heidegger or Walter Friedrich Otto) approved Nietzsche's annexation by the Third Reich, if only temporarily and officially, not because they had been 'misled' by Nietzsche's sister but, as Erich F. Podach has rightly observed, from personal conviction.[10] It is no coincidence that the best books written on Nietzsche in this period were the work of opponents of National Socialism, such as Karl Löwith, Erich F. Podach, Karl Jaspers and Edgar Salin.

2. In his unforgettable essay on Hofmannsthal and his age, Hermann Broch defined Nietzsche as the only thinker of the last century who had been cognizant of the 'collapse of values'.[11] In reality, Nietzsche's philosophy reflects the radical end of religious and metaphysical illusions; it is only in Nietzsche that the Christian God is truly dead, and with him the moral values of Christianity. Nietzsche is not unaware of the social or (in a broad sense) the political origins of moral valuations. But he makes the error of believing that modern socialism is nothing but a continuation of Christianity. Nietzsche thus combats the sort of *tartufferie* that proclaims the equality of all men as a 'moral aim'. Nietzsche did not know Marx and Engels's polemic against equality as a petit-bourgeois catchword, which resonated within the ranks of German social democracy and within European socialism generally. Thus, he hardly ever managed to escape the moralistic dimension of passing judgement upon the most important politico-cultural

---

10 Erich F. Podach, *Friedrich Nietzsches Werke des Zusammenbruchs* (Heidelberg: Rothe, 1961).

11 Hermann Broch, 'Hofmannsthal und seine Zeit', *Essays*, vol. l (Zurich: Rhein Verlag, 1955), 43–182; *Hugo von Hofmannsthal and His Time: The European Imagination, 1860–1920*, ed. and trans. Michael P. Steinberg (Chicago, IL: University of Chicago Press, 1984).

phenomenon of his time, socialism, seeing in it only a manifestation of 'ressentiment' similar to that of the Christians who, in the ancient world, had destroyed Greco-Roman culture. He therefore lacked the most elementary knowledge for correctly evaluating the theory of socialism. It was simple for the socialist theorists of the generation following Marx to dismiss Nietzsche as a petit-bourgeois apologist for capitalist exploitation. But these theorists, in turn, reduced (and continue to reduce) the entire philosophy of this greatest destroyer of myths, whom we have here tried to expound in all his complexity and with due regard to his problematic nature, to politics, as if politics exhausted the entire sphere of human activity. The fact that Nietzsche's critique was directed against any attempt to condemn human reality by moral standards seems to have escaped all his Marxist interpreters, from Mehring to Lukács. Here, it is not a question of wanting to 'recover Nietzsche for democracy and socialism', as some have said even recently, but rather of asserting that, even within a socialist and democratic society (or within the movement that could lead to one), we cannot do without a 'Nietzsche dimension' – that is, without the dimension of mental freedom born of the critical, rational and liberatory potential of his thought, which never tires of putting everything into question. This also permits us to ask whether the individual (even in a society of presumptive equals) properly finds his defence and his own field of spontaneous activity in the realm of culture (as Burckhardt also understood it), and, in the last analysis, *against the state* – provided that one believes in the necessary extinction of the state in the 'reign of freedom', and that one thus really desires the overcoming of 'politics' as repression.

Appendix
Goethe's Pupil: Notes on Nietzsche and Thomas Mann (1975)

If I might be allowed to begin by enunciating three deliberately provocative theses:[1]

I. No thinker and writer exerted a more enduring influence on Thomas Mann than Nietzsche did. I would add that this Nietzsche was and always remained for Mann primarily 'Goethe's pupil'.

II. Any analysis of Mann's relationship to Nietzsche must necessarily be supported with detailed philological and historical work. This means, on the one hand, that the countless allusions to and citations from Nietzsche hidden in Mann's literary writings require investigation, and, on the other hand, that beyond direct reading – and Mann was an excellent reader of Nietzsche – there was a conventional image of Nietzsche, a 'mythical' Nietzsche, or, rather, a 'myth' of Nietzsche, that conditioned Mann's views considerably. It will suffice in this regard to recall the so-called great biography written by Elisabeth Förster-Nietzsche, of unblessèd memory, and the mythological imposture of Ernst Bertram (a pendant work, let

1 The appendix was originally published as Mazzino Montinari, 'Lo scolaro di Goethe', *Su Nietzsche* (Rome: Editori Riuniti, 1981), 66–72.

us recall, to Mann's *Reflections of an Unpolitical Man*). We must therefore make a distinction between the Nietzsche who was a direct factor in Mann's intellectual formation or *Bildungserlebnis* and a mythical Nietzsche who could be (and in some cases did become) an object of further mythmaking, in Mann's work as well.

III. In my view, examining the relationship between Nietzsche and Thomas Mann historically and philologically entails abandoning the pretence of situating the two authors ideologically. Above all, it requires that we not attempt to set Thomas Mann within a historical schema of redemption, which would have him developing to the point of foreseeing the 'magnificent and progressive destiny' of humanity as it progressed toward socialism, or – at the very least – one in which, under the aegis of Goethe, he gradually emancipated himself from the maleficent influence of Nietzsche. This 'providential' schema does not permit us to grasp the individual historical specificity either of Thomas Mann or of Nietzsche. The best method is to consider Mann and Nietzsche and their relationship as elements of the sphere that defines itself – in contradistinction to the sphere of the state, or, more broadly, to the political sphere and the sphere of religious and ideological convictions and institutions with which it comprises a historical totality – as culture, in Jacob Burckhardt's sense of the term. We must not lose the capacity to make distinctions; otherwise, instead of writing history – that is, seeking out the typical in order to arrive at a genuine understanding of a given phenomenon (in this case, Thomas Mann's relationship to Nietzsche) – we will end by reducing everything to a preconceived view that, ultimately, requires no verification.

I would like to focus on a few significant statements by Thomas Mann regarding Nietzsche, taken from his later essayistic works, but not from the *Reflections of an Unpolitical Man*, where Nietzsche's presence makes itself felt from the title to the final page, and where we also find the strongest support for our thesis regarding the particular sphere within which we must situate Mann's relationship to Nietzsche: namely in its argument for the defence of the spirit and of art against politics, which is still to be found in the lecture 'My Times' of May 1950. In this late lecture we learn that, when Mann distances himself from the *Reflections*, he is not distancing himself from Nietzsche, who is defined here, in 1950 (NB *after* the earlier lecture of 1947 on Nietzsche's philosophy, which might have led superficial interpreters to think that Mann meant to put behind him much of his Nietzschean experience), as a 'humanist even in his most strident and painful eccentricities' who put 'at the centre of his own philosophy the elevation of man and of his future, freed from moral humiliations'.

When, four years after publishing the *Reflections*, Thomas Mann found himself defending the democratic Weimar Republic, without 'noticing any fracture' in his existence and 'without the least impression of having had to renounce anything', he understood himself – faced with the antihumanism of the time – as never having done (or at least never having wanted to do) anything other than to defend *Humanität* (humanity, humanism). But, from this point onward, his defence of *Humanität* was also conducted in the spirit of Nietzsche, and thus Thomas Mann was one of the first in Germany to recognize that the reactionary right was getting ready to annex Nietzsche, and to falsify him. In this regard, we would recall the memorable words that Mann wrote in opposition to Alfred Bäumler, a proponent of the reactionary interpretation of Nietzsche, in 1927. Likewise, two years later, in his lecture on Lessing of 1929, Mann spoke of the all-too-common spectacle in aid of which '*der schlechte und schlichte Un- und Antigeist*' (plain and simple un- and anti-intelligence)[2] seeks to

2 Thomas Mann, *Essays of Three Decades*, translated by H. T. Lowe-Porter (New York: Alfred A. Knopf, 1947), 199.

appropriate, while falsifying, the products of the intellect, so as to adorn itself with them. For Thomas Mann, Nietzsche's 'prophecy' is 'drunkenness of the spirit', and Nietzsche's hostility toward the spirit, his anti-idealism, is only one aspect of this. Let us then take for granted that Mann has no intention of renouncing the heritage of Nietzsche, even in his period of being a '*Wanderredner*', an 'itinerant preacher', of democracy.

This assertion is confirmed once again by the lecture on 'Goethe as Representative of the Bourgeois Age', of 1932. By this time, Thomas Mann was fighting his final battles on behalf of democracy and the Weimar Republic: defeat was on the horizon. But here as well, he calls on Nietzsche as an ally against the National Socialist *Ungeist* (un-intellect, negation of the intellect). The passsage is well known, but it is worth rereading:

> Goethe, Schopenhauer, Wagner, Nietzsche – there it is, the firmament of our youth with its fixed stars . . . the bourgeois intellectual world, which precisely as a world of the mind is an extra-bourgeois one and leads, through Nietzsche, Goethe's pupil, into new, post-bourgeois, still nameless future worlds . . . The will and the vocation to the utmost abrogation of the bourgeois [*Entbürgerlichung*], the highly dangerous adventure of the aspiring thought [in German: *das Abenteuer des versuchenden Gedankens*], that is the passport [*der Freibrief*] which intellect itself has offered to the man of the bourgeoisie. That son and grandson of Protestant clergymen, in whom the romanticism of the nineteenth century achieved the conquest of itself, whose martyr's death on the cross of thought broke a path to the unspeakably new, Friedrich Nietzsche: where did his roots lie, if not in the soil of bourgeois humanity? And just such a self-overcoming of the bourgeois by the power of

intellect we find in the novel of Goethe's old age, the *Wanderjahre*.[3]

Here Mann understands Nietzsche's overcoming of romanticism in analogy to the overcoming of the bourgeois element in Goethe's *Wilhelm Meister*, and defines Nietzsche as 'Goethe's pupil'. Indeed, it would seem he includes *Entbürgerlichung* (de-bourgeoisification) in Nietzsche's overcoming of romanticism. In this way, Goethe's pupil represents the transition to new, still nameless post-bourgeois worlds.

In another work of the Goethe-year 1932, 'Goethe's Career as a Man of Letters', Goethe and Nietzsche are united by their critique of the Germans: and, here, the philologist might be permitted to emphasize that Mann is entirely correct to note the Goethean traits in Nietzsche's critiques of Germany. One could cite innumerable 'Goethean' passages in Nietzsche's published and posthumous writings. What is more, Mann recognizes with a sure instinct that Nietzsche's prose style is based on Goethe's, just as Goethe's is based on Luther's. Mann spoke explicitly of a Luther-Goethe-Nietzsche lineage: 'The master-pupil relationship is as clear between Goethe and Nietzsche as it is between Luther and Goethe.'[4] And, in this context, he could not ignore the other great writer of nineteenth-century German prose: 'On the whole, we may envisage Nietzsche's, indeed even Heine's relation to Goethe as psychologist and stylist in the same light as that of Goethe to Luther, and we may rejoice over the progressive refinement of the German essence, or lament over it as decay.'[5] What a history of literature there is in these lines! They

3 Ibid., 89–90.

4 Ibid., 60 [translation modified].

5 Ibid.

also recall the proximity of the *Reflections of an Unpolitical Man* to Heine's book on Ludwig Börne, which was in its way equally a claim on behalf of culture over against the State, and even against revolution.

The witness who Thomas Mann invokes at decisive moments to define his relationship to Schopenhauer and Wagner, the other fixed stars of his youth, is always Nietzsche. But, even for Goethe, we find – in the great essay 'Goethe and Tolstoy' of 1922, whose subtitle is 'Fragments on the Problem of Humanism' – a page in which Mann returns at some length to Nietzsche, when, once again, he would define Goethe's alleged paganism so as to prevent its possible annexation by National Socialist and antihumanist ideology. 'Nietzsche,' Mann writes, 'placed Goethe, historically and psychologically, between "Hellenism and Pietism", and thus expressed the combination of creative and critical, naive and sentimental [Schiller's terms, as is well known], ancient and modern in Goethe's character. In fact,' Mann continues, 'Goethe's "Pietism" is nothing other than his modernity. Many centuries of Christian cultivation of interiority and a whole century of autobiographical exercises in Pietistic self-analysis were needed to make possible a work like *Werther*.'[6]

As for Wagner and Schopenhauer, in 1938 Thomas Mann – in his essay on the pessimistic philosopher – was able to say what many interpreters of Nietzsche have not sufficiently understood, when he defined the manner in which Nietzsche distanced himself from Wagner and Schopenhauer as 'a great and decisive event in the history of the intellect'.[7] At the same time, Mann highlights the continuity of Nietzsche's development, noting Wagner's

6 Ibid., 138 [translation modified].

7 Ibid., 374.

continuing presence up to the famous pages on *Tristan* in *Ecce Homo* and a 'continuation and interpretation of the Schopenhauerian image of the world' in Nietzsche's philosophy.[8] But, precisely in writing the essay on Schopenhauer, Thomas Mann felt the need to guard against a possible fatal confusion provoked by Nietzsche's exaltation of 'life' over against Schopenhauer's pessimism. 'It would be hard to assert that Nietzsche's Dionysiac, anti-Christian enthusiasm was personally something healthier and more robust than Schopenhauer's resentment against life – or that, objectively or intellectually, he brought more health into the world. Nietzsche worked far too much, and in a confusing way, with this biological contrast, summoning up a false idea of health which is now trampling on the spiritual factor that might today [in 1938] heal Europe. But he himself indicates a step further in suffering, in subtlety and modernity – particularly in the quality in which, more explicitly than any other, he is the pupil of Schopenhauer – I mean as a psychologist.'[9] For those who are familiar with the foolish Nazi tirades *à la* Bäumler that refused to recognize Nietzsche as a psychologist in favour of imagining him as a politician, the intention of these lines of Mann's is clear. A few lines down, in fact, as on prior occasions (for example 'Freud and the Future', 1936) and later as well, Mann traces another line of modern thought: the one which, beginning with Schopenhauer and passing through the decisive stage of Nietzsche, arrives at the psychoanalysis of Sigmund Freud. 'In Nietzsche's aphoristic writings, Freudian revelations are anticipated as if by a flash of lightning.'[10] It would seem no one can doubt this today.

---

8 Ibid., 374 [translation modified].

9 Ibid., 407–8 [translation modified].

10 Ibid., 408.

Without multiplying the examples, we can say that Thomas Mann's reckoning with Nietzsche, the inward debate with this teacher of his, runs through the totality of Mann's essayistic work, his letters, all his poetic creations. This reckoning found its grandiose coronation in that work of his most extreme maturity, *Doctor Faustus*, whose title suggests the close presence of that other master of Mann's, Goethe.

Here, Nietzsche's destiny is inextricably intertwined with that of Germany and of Thomas Mann himself. The 'Nietzsche myth', more than the *Bildungserlebnis* Nietzsche, is subjected to an extreme intensification and radicalization. This should not be forgotten. But here we need more than ever to apply the art of distinction and interpretation that Nietzsche called 'slow reading'. It would, in fact, be naive, indeed anti-historical, to deny that the facts reveal a deep connection not only between the 'myth of Nietzsche' or the 'mythical Nietzsche' and the suicide of German culture and Nazi barbarism, but also between a certain authentically Nietzschean intellectual cruelty and its coarse simplification in the hands of the Hitlerites. Thus, Mann attempted an explanation from inside in the form of a reckoning with the fate of Leverkühn-Nietzsche, understood as a symbol of Germany's nihilistic catastrophe.

Several passages from letters Mann wrote in this period are interesting in this context. The lecture on 'Nietzsche's Philosophy in Light of Recent Experience' (1947) is quickly followed by a conspicuous tendency to recalibrate the significance of Nietzsche's philosophy for Mann's own relationship to Nietzsche. In a letter to his brother Heinrich he defines it as *simpel*, simple-minded; to another correspondent Mann confesses to having tried to maintain an equilibrium between 'critique and veneration'. To Emil Preetorius he writes of a failure to measure up to his own ambitions with regard to his desire to plumb the depths of Nietzsche's heart: 'The essay on Nietzsche, let me repeat once again, is not what I myself nor perhaps others expected of me on the subject. It is the Faustus novel more than anything else.' Eventually, Mann loses patience, writing on 26 December 1947 to Maximilian Brantl, who seems to have been dissatisfied with this essay because of how in the end it effectively redeems Nietzsche rather too much:

> 'O, what a *noble* mind is here o'erthrown.' The motto is appropriate, and you need not lament that I failed to indicate all the destruction and the destructiveness. Nor must you hold against me my enduring veneration for a peerless intensification of language, for the practically unprecedented richness of spirit and piercing insight that abound in his early books, and for the dramatic spectacle of a life of such mythical and awe-inspiring grandeur. 'A great man is a public misfortune,' say the Chinese. A German great man especially. But wasn't Luther a misfortune? *And wasn't Goethe*? Look closely: what Nietzschean immoralism there is hidden in his nature-worshipping anti-moralism! Back then, in Goethe's time, everything could still be beautiful, serene and classical. Then it became grotesque, drunk, agonizing as a crucifixion, and also criminal. Such are the times, such is the spirit, such is fate . . . I cannot be angry with Nietzsche because 'my dear Germans have ruined him for me'. If they have been so stupid as to have been seduced by his diabolism, that's their problem, and if they cannot tolerate their great men, then they shouldn't make any more of them.

In his 'Fantasy on Goethe' of 1948, Mann cannot help but return once again to Nietzsche the 'pupil', writing:

> The aloofness of artistic as well as natural creations from all purpose [*Zweckfremdheit*] was Goethe's highest principle, and

> he regarded his innate poetic talent as 'entirely nature', a gift of the all-beneficent mother [*allgütige Mutter*], who holds both good and evil alike in her embrace. In this lie the roots of his youthful enthusiasm for Shakespeare. Goethe's aestheticism of nature and antimoralism was subsequently to influence Nietzsche, the immoralist, who was destined to take a further step and rapturously proclaim the primacy of evil over good, the former's overwhelming importance for the preservation and triumph of life.[11]

Mann notes in this essay as well that another Goethean element, antipathy to the Cross, was driven to the point of paroxysm in 'Nietzsche's feverish diatribes against the religion of loving-kindness'.[12]

Finally, the essay 'On Schiller', written in the year of Mann's death (1955), includes a reference to Nietzsche bearing on the key matter of illness: 'His was an accommodation to illness, an adjustment to living at peace with it. In his intellectual pride Schiller would scarcely alllow it to shadow his gaiety and audacity. Indeed, he occasionally expressed his gratitude to it, just as Nietzsche did.'[13]

11 Thomas Mann, *Last Essays*, translated by Richard and Clara Winston and Tania and James Stern (New York: Alfred A. Knopf, 1966), 120-1.

12 Ibid., 126.

13 Ibid., 55.

Index of Names

Index of Nietzsche's Works